SCIENTIFIC EYE

Exploring the Marvels of Science

■ ■ ■ ■ ■

Adam Hart-Davis

 Sterling Publishing Co., Inc.   New York

Library of Congress Cataloging-in-Publication Data

Hart-Davis, Adam.
  The scientific eye : exploring the marvels of science / by Adam Hart-Davis.
    p. cm.
  Includes index.
  Summary: Introduces basic scientific principles accompanied by related riddles and jokes.
  ISBN 0-8069-6920-2
  1. Science—Miscellanea—Juvenile literature. 2. Science—Philosophy—Juvenile literature. [1. Science—Miscellanea.
2. Science—Wit and humor. 3. Riddles. 4. Jokes.] I. Title.
Q173.H315 1989
500—dc19   88-31333
                                                                CIP
                                                                 AC

Published in 1989 by Sterling Publishing Co., Inc.
Two Park Avenue, New York, New York 10016.
Distributed in Canada by Oak Tree Press Ltd.
% Canadian Manda Group, P.O. Box 920, Station U,
Toronto, Ontario, Canada M8Z 5P9

Originally published under the title *The Scientific Eye* by Unwin Hyman Limited, London, © 1985 Adam Hart-Davis.

American adaptation by Sterling Publishing Co., Inc., and Adam Hart-Davis, © 1989 by Adam Hart-Davis.

The jokes and riddles in this adaptation have been taken from or are based upon Joseph Rosenbloom's *Funniest Dinosaur Book Ever!, Giggles, Gags & Groaners, The Zaniest Riddle Book in the World, The Mad Scientist, Gigantic Joke Book, The Biggest Riddle Book in the World* © Joseph Rosenbloom 1987, 1987, 1984, 1982, 1978, 1976, respectively, all published by Sterling Publishing Co., Inc. and used by permission.

Contents

Acknowledgments

The author would like to acknowledge that the ideas in this book came from a variety of sources, including David Attenborough's *Life on Earth*, Michael Faraday's *The Chemical History of a Candle*, Desmond Morris's *The Naked Ape*, and the BBC-TV Horizon program, *The Life That Lives on Man*. Many people made positive suggestions about what I should do with the text. Those who were particularly helpful in shaping it include David Edwards, Jo Heys, David Jones, Christopher Kington, Robert Moss, Antonia Murphy, Margaret Sands, David Waddington, John Walker, Martin Ward and Simon Welfare. Thank you all.

The photographs come from: Natural History Photographic Agency, 7; Met Office, 24; Dr. Y. Furukawa, 24; Dr. Charles Knight, 24; Science Photo Library, 33; Zoological Society of London, 33; Ministry of Agriculture, Fisheries & Food, 33, 43; Biofotos, 41; Natural History Museum, 41; Royal Veterinary College, 43; all other photographs from Adam Hart-Davis.

The Scientific Eye television series is a Yorkshire Television production. Executive Producer: Chris Jelley. Producer: Adam Hart-Davis. Director: Michael Cocker.

Why bother with science?

Why does the best bubble-gum bubble better than the second-best bubble-gum? Are bubble-gum scientists studying the bubbles using all the latest instruments? Perhaps when they understand more clearly how bubble-gum works, they may be able to make it bubble better.

Scientists are people who try to understand how things work.

Science is what they use to try and understand.

The scientific method

Suppose that outside a school there were suddenly several accidents in which students were knocked down by cars. How could they be stopped? Many suggestions could be made. How can you tell which is right?

This doesn't sound like a scientific problem, but you can try to solve it by using the **scientific method**. Science is not just about experiments. Science is a way of looking at the world. Science is about bubble-gum and balloons and bananas. People who think like scientists have a particular way of looking at the world and at its problems.

The **first** part of the scientific method is to gather information. **Second**, sort it out, or *analyze* it. **Third**, guess what is going on. **Fourth**, test your guess with one or more experiments.

What was the information about the accidents outside the school? It turned out that they all happened at the same time of day—during morning break. And there was a new ice-cream truck that had begun parking opposite the school.

Now you are able to guess what was happening. Students were running across the road to get to the ice-cream truck. The solution was simple. The driver was asked to park on the same side of the road as the school.

This solution was tested by watching for further accidents. No more were reported. The solution was successful.

Remember the scientific method: observe, analyze, come up with a theory, test it by experiment. Or, if you like: **Look, Think, Guess, Try**.

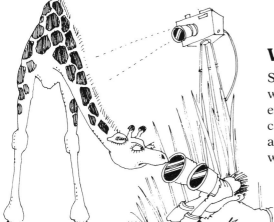

What do scientists do?

Some people think that a scientist is a person who wears a white coat and talks about experiments. Well, some scientists do. Others climb mountains, go to Africa to look for strange animals, do delicate brain surgery, or work out ways of producing more food.

Two black cats want to get through a door. The door is slightly open, but it opens towards them; so when they push they can't get through. Sam, the stupid cat, sits there and mews, in the hope that someone will come and open the door. But Booboo does not give up so easily. He pushes his nose through, and then his paw, trying to reach outside. And soon he finds that if he puts his paw through and pulls, he can open the door.

You couldn't call Booboo a scientist. His method is mainly trial and error. But he does solve problems and try to understand his environment. That is what science is all about.

The point of reading this book is to find out about thinking scientifically. Reading it won't turn you into a scientist, but it will help you to look at the world with a scientific eye.

1. Averages, pies, and bars

Suppose you have chosen a problem to study. The first stage of the scientific process is watching. You need to gather information before you can do anything else. And what you usually gather is a whole load of numbers. What scientists often need is a way to make sense of these numbers.

Averages

Suppose you asked all the girls in your class how long it takes to walk to school in the morning. Their answers, in minutes, are 3, 8, 24, 7, 14, 30, 12, 9, 10, and 33.

Now you can guess that they don't all walk at the same speed. And some will have farther to walk than others. But you can get a general idea of how long it takes a girl to walk to school from the **average** time. You get the average by adding all the answers together, and then dividing by the number of answers.

$$\text{Average} = \frac{\textbf{Sum of all answers added together}}{\textbf{Number of answers}}$$

In this case there are ten girls, and the average time they take to walk to school is

$$\frac{3+8+24+7+14+30+12+9+10+33}{10} = \frac{150}{10} \text{ or } 15 \text{ minutes}$$

Notice that none of the girls takes exactly 15 minutes. The average number does not have to be one of the answers.

If you drink one glass of milk every day, and your friend drinks three, what is the average number of glasses of milk drunk every day?

Total number of glasses of milk = 4
Total number of milk drinkers = 2
Average = 4/2 = 2 glasses of milk every day

8

pepperoni — 15
extra cheese — 8
mushroom — 6
anchovy — 1
─────
30

Pies

Pie charts are a splendid way of displaying information. Suppose you went around the whole class and asked everyone "What's your favorite kind of pizza?" The answers are 15 pepperoni or sausage, 8 extra cheese, 6 mushroom, and 1 anchovy.

You now want to show what fraction of the class likes each type flavor. Draw a **pie chart**. The pie stands for the whole class. Exactly half the class (15 out of 30) like pepperoni or sausage, so color half the pie for pepperoni or sausage. Just over half of the rest like extra cheese, so color them a thick slice. One fifth of the class like mushroom, so color them a thin slice. And color a tiny piece for the one who likes anchovy. Color the small slices the darkest, so you can see them.

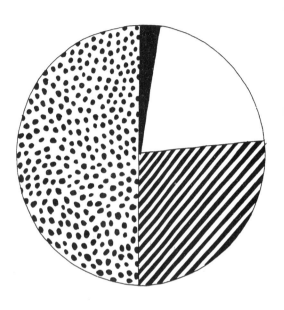

Bars

Bar charts are better than pies when you have numbers to deal with.

How many bananas do the boys in your class eat in a week? First make a table with "number of bananas" across the top and "number of boys" up the side. Go around and ask each boy how many bananas he eats, and fill in the table. Then make a bar chart just like the table, but using colored bars instead of checks. From the chart you can see right away which is the most common number, and how many boys eat very few bananas.

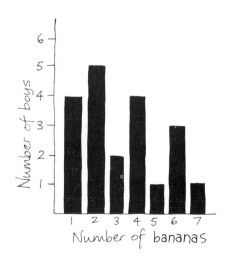

9

2. Mass meeting

If you turn into a ghost, *mass* is what you'll miss the most.

Harry Martindale was fixing pipes in a cellar in his house. Suddenly, he says, he heard a trumpet blast. He looked down and saw a Roman soldier walk out of the wall.

Terrified, he fell off his ladder and hid at the back of the cellar. As he watched, a large shaggy horse came through the wall, with another soldier riding it. Then out marched a whole column of Roman soldiers, helmets shining. They wore leather vests, faded green skirts, and short swords.

The strangest thing was that he could not see their legs below the knees. Later he found that the old Roman road ran about a foot and a half below the cellar floor.

Harry was scared stiff that the soldiers would see him and cut him to pieces. But he didn't have to worry. Like all good ghosts, those Roman soldiers had no mass.

What is mass?

Mass is the amount of stuff in an object. A massive object has a lot of mass in it.

We measure mass in tons, pounds, and ounces.

1 ton = 2,000 lbs.   1 lb. = 16 oz.

You can't push a pencil through your desk, because the stuff of the pencil bashes into the stuff of the desk. But if the pencil had no mass it would have no stuff, and it could go through the desk. Harry's Roman soldiers were able to march through the wall because they had no mass. And so they could not have hurt him with their swords. The swords would have gone through him, but he would not have felt a thing!

Why mass matters

What can hurt you is to run into someone or something at full speed. If you dash along the corridor at school, and crash into someone in your class, who would hurt you most? The smallest or the biggest in the class?

You would knock the smallest person flying. But if you smacked into the biggest you might get really hurt. Why? Because the biggest person in the class is the most massive. In a crash, the more the mass, the bigger the bang.

RIDICULOUS RIDDLES

What happens when two oxen crash into each other?
They have an ox-ident.

What people travel the most?
Romans.

How do we know Rome was built at night?
Because Rome wasn't built in a day.

What do you get when you cross the Roman army and a ghost?
A big nothing.

3. Weight and see

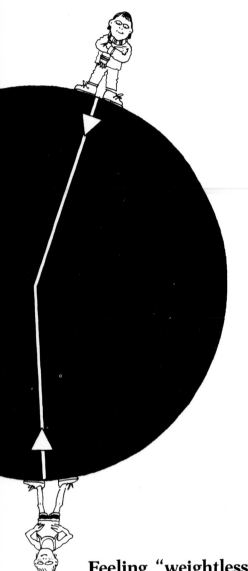

Weight is different from mass.

Your mass is the amount of stuff in your body. The mass of the Earth is the amount of stuff in the Earth. The mass of the Earth pulls your mass down. What you feel is **weight**.

Your weight is the pull of the Earth's mass on your mass.

Wherever you are on Earth, your weight is a downward pull—never upward or sideways. Down means towards the middle of the Earth.

How to lose weight

Your mass is the same wherever you are, but your weight may be different in different places. Climb a high mountain and you will weigh a little less. Why? Because you are farther from the center of the Earth. Your mass is pulled down less hard.

On the Moon you would weigh only about one-sixth of what you weigh on Earth. Take a look at the chart on the next page. It shows what you'd weigh on each planet (plus Sun and Moon) if you weighed 100 pounds on Earth. For the greatest weight loss, go to Pluto.

Feeling "weightless"

Astronauts feel "weightless" as they orbit around the Earth. You can get this "weightless" feeling too.

Get a string about a yard long and hang a roll of cellophane tape in the middle of it. Stand on a table. In each hand hold one end of the string. Keep your arms straight. Start with the string stretched tight. Then bring your hands together. The string will sag as the weight of the tape pulls it down.

Now do it again, but this time jump off the table just before you clap your hands together. Jump upwards off the table so that you are in the air as long as possible. Clap your hands together while you are on the way down. The string will not sag. You will catch the tape. While you are falling, both you and the tape seem to have no weight.

Gravity

Any two lumps of stuff in the Universe are being pulled towards each other all the time. This pull is called **gravity**. The Earth has a huge mass, and so its gravity is usually the biggest pull on your body. This pull of gravity is what gives you weight. The reason you weigh only one sixth of what you weigh on the Earth when you're on the Moon is that gravity is six times smaller there.

Not much gravity up here

MOON

ON YOUR WEIGH!

If you weighed 100 pounds on Earth, here's what you'd weigh on the Sun, Moon and planets:

Sun	2,790 pounds
Moon	17 pounds
Mercury	38 pounds
Venus	91 pounds
Mars	38 pounds
Jupiter	254 pounds
Saturn	108 pounds
Uranus	91 pounds
Neptune	119 pounds
Pluto	5 pounds*

*****Approx. The mass of Pluto is not known.**

To get your exact weight on any of these places, multiply your weight by the number of pounds shown above. Then put a decimal point two digits from the right. For example, if you weigh 50 pounds, and you want to know your weight on Mars, multiply:

$$38 \times 50 = 1900$$

and put in the decimal point:

$$19.00$$

The answer is 19 pounds.

4. May the force be with you

If you want to move a mountain, or a molehill, or a horse—when the bottle of ketchup is blocked with red sauce, and you want things to move—then you need to use force.

Force makes things move

Forces move things. Nothing can *begin* to move unless a force starts it. Forces may push, pull, tug, heave, squeeze, stretch, twist, or press, but what they all do is move things.

Weight is a force. Your mass is pulled down by gravity. The result of that pull is the force we call weight. Does this force make you move? Yes. Step off a chair, and the force will pull you quickly to the floor. Sit at the top of a slide in the playground, and the force will pull you down.

Sit on a springy bench, and the bench will bend under your weight. The force of your weight pulls you down until the bench has bent enough to hold you. The more mass you have, the bigger your weight, and the more you will bend the bench.

WEIGHT

FORCE

SQUEEZE

PRESS

PUSH

BEND

FLATTEN

When does the bench stop bending? When the forces balance. The bench is springy. It pushes upwards on you. The more it bends, the harder it pushes. When the push of the bench is exactly equal to your weight, the bench will stop bending.

How do we measure force?

Forces are measured in newtons. If you hang a 1-pound mass on a piece of string, it will pull on the string with a force of 4.45 newtons—nearly 4½ newtons.

Weight is a force. If your mass is 90 pounds, then your weight is over 400 newtons.

Remember: Forces move things. If something isn't moving, then the forces on it are exactly balanced.

PUSHY RIDDLES

How do you make a lemon drop?
Let go of it.

NIP: Did your mother ever lift weights?
TUCK: What made you think that?
NIP: How else could she have raised a big dumbbell like you?

How do you make hamburger roll?
Give it a push.

What shellfish make the best weight-lifters?
Mussels.

5. Science friction

Why do gym shoes have rubber soles? To help stop you slipping on the floor. Rubber doesn't slip easily on a wooden floor, because of **friction**. Friction helps you to stop slipping.

When one thing slides over another—like a foot over the floor—friction is a force that tries to stop it. The size of this force depends on the floor, and on the shoes. Leather is more slippery than rubber, unless the floor is wet.

The force of friction is greater for things that are heavier. You can see this with a pair of walking legs.

Walking legs

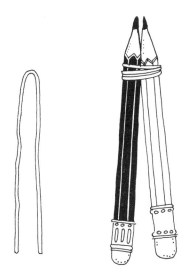

Make a pair of legs by bending a large paper clip into a narrow U-shape. Or take two pencils with erasers on the ends for feet. Use a rubber band to tie the pencils together, near their points, to make a narrow V-shape.

Hold a ruler on its edge on a desk or table. Stand the pencil legs on either side of the ruler. Let them lean on it at an angle, with both feet on the desk.

Lift the ruler up half an inch or so, and then let it down again. Keep doing this, and the legs will walk along the ruler. They walk better on a rough surface. Try walking them on this book if the desk is too slippery.

Here you see it with the paper clip:

In this picture, the ruler is going down. The feet take on the weight. Friction is high at the feet, but low at the bend in the paper clip. So the bend slides, but the feet do not.

Here the ruler is going up. The bend in the paper clip is where the weight is. Friction is high there. Little weight is on the feet; so friction is low, and the feet slide easily.

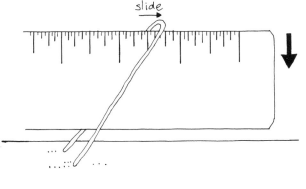

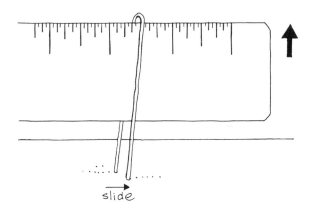

Making more friction

Some new bottle tops are screwed on much too tight. Often you can't get into the Coke, or the peanut butter jar. The top just slips around in your hand. What you need is *more friction*.

Some people use a dish towel, but old rubber kitchen gloves are better. Cut a finger off the glove to slip over a bottle top. Slip the wrist part over a jar top. The rubber glove will create more friction. You will get a better grip on the top, and you should be able to unscrew it.

Making less friction

Old bicycles squeak and stick. This means there is too much friction. Put a drop of oil in the right place and the bike should run smoothly again. Sticking is caused by friction. Oil reduces friction. Oil is a **lubricant**.

Wet soap is also a lubricant. Have you ever dropped the soap in the shower or in the bath? It's hard to pick up, because it's so slippery. If you step on a piece of wet soap, you'll probably fall flat on your face!

Banana skins are even more slippery than oil or wet soap. The outside of a banana skin is like rubber—not slippery at all. But the inside has a thick layer of sugary paste. This paste is very slippery indeed. If you step on the inside you will almost certainly slip.

But, what's even worse is to tread on the outside. Then the inside of the skin will slide on the floor. If you tread on the inside you can skid only the length of the skin—8 inches or so. But if you tread on a banana skin slippery side down, you could skid a long way. . . .

6. How dense are you?

Which weighs more, a pound of feathers or a pound of gold? The answer is that they weigh exactly the same amount, for they both have the same mass, 1 lb. The difference is that a 1 lb. bar of gold would be about the size of half a Mars bar, but 1 lb. of feathers would fill a pillow.

The gold packs its 1 lb. mass into a much smaller volume than the feathers. We say that gold is much more **dense**. This means that a small volume of gold has a large mass.

Heavy in your hands

See if you can find a few different kinds of materials: some blocks of wood, iron (or metal weights), polystyrene or foam rubber, lead, gold jewelry or coins, and cork. Handle them, and see if you can figure out which are the heaviest and which are the lightest.

Polystyrene and cork feel light. Metals feel heavy. This is because metals are more dense.

Gold is much denser than lead, but not the densest stuff in the world. A poisonous metal called osmium is even denser. But osmium doesn't look or sound as good as gold. No one has made a film called "Osmiumfinger"!

Range of densities
From: Empty space
  Polystyrene
  Cork
  Wood
  Water
  Stone
  Iron
  Lead
  Gold
  Osmium

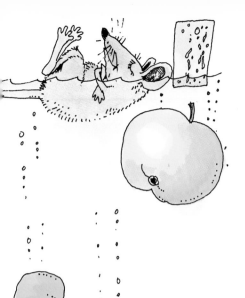

If sharks don't swim, they sink

Anything will float in water if its density is less than the density of water. Wood floats. Metal sinks.

Fruit and vegetables are mostly water, and they usually *just* sink or *just* float. Try this at home with a bowl of water. You will probably find that apples, oranges, and bananas float, but carrots and tomatoes sink. Oranges sometimes sink when they are peeled; the fruit is denser than the peel.

Animals are also mostly water. But animals have a layer of fat under the skin, and air spaces inside, like lungs. So most animals *just* float in water. When you lie back in a swimming pool your face should float above the surface. But fish have to stay under water. Their life would become terrible if they kept bobbing up like corks! Sharks are denser than water. If they don't keep swimming they sink to the bottom.

DANGER

What is yellow, smooth and very dense?
Shark-infested custard.

What do you get if you cross a shark and a parrot?
An animal that talks your ear off.

Is it dangerous to swim on a full stomach?
It's better to swim on water.

MORE DANGER

What is that soft, mushy stuff between a shark's teeth?
Slow swimmers.

What is the difference between a shark and peanut butter?
The shark doesn't stick to the roof of your mouth.

7. The skin on the water

There's a funny little insect called the water strider. It has short front legs, and it runs around on top of the water. The water strider is not heavy at all. But even so you might expect its feet to sink into the water.

There is also a lizard about 4 inches long which dashes across the water. It runs furiously across, as if it isn't quite sure whether it can reach the other side without sinking.

Why don't they sink?

For the water strider and the little lizard, water behaves as though it had a skin on the surface. The creatures' legs press a little way into this skin, but don't go through. Instead the skin bends down for them. What you can see is an example of the **surface tension** of the water.

It's as if the surface of the water is pulling inwards, and it doesn't want to be broken.

You can see this clearly when you float a paper clip on the surface of water. Take a dry paper clip. Make a small shovel from a square of paper towel or toilet paper. Use the shovel to place the paper clip carefully and gently on the top of the water in a glass or cup. Then carefully use another paper clip or a pencil to poke the paper away and leave the paper clip floating by itself.

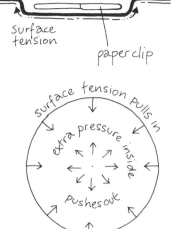

surface
tension

paper clip

surface tension pulls in

extra pressure inside

pushes out

The paper clip has a much greater density than the water. Obviously, it should sink at once. It floats only because of this curious surface tension. Look at the photograph. You can see how the weight of the paper clip bends the surface of the water. The water surface behaves like a stretched rubber blanket pushing up on the metal.

Smooth water

Have you noticed the smoothness of water when it runs from a tap? It looks like a smooth round rope, or like smooth round drops. *Always round. Always smooth.* Because the surface tension pulls it *inwards*.

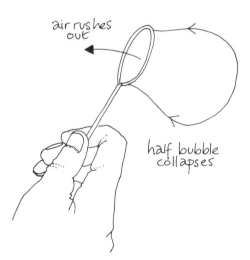

air rushes
out

half bubble
collapses

Bubbles are also smooth and round. A bubble is a bundle of gas pulled together by a skin of water. The volume of the bubble is determined by the gas inside. The shape is affected by the skin. The skin of water pulls the bubble into the shape that has the smallest surface area—a sphere. So the roundness of the bubble shows the tension in the surface.

Prepare a bubble mixture from soap and water (use about 8 tablespoons of water for every tablespoon of soap). Put the bubble mixture on a wire loop, blow the bubble halfway up, and then stop. What happens? The bubble blows back at you. Try it and see.

Surface tension is always trying to make a bubble smaller. In this case it is possible. The bubbles gets smaller by blowing air out in your face.

Two Martians landed in the Atlantic Ocean. One said, "Hey, man, look at all that water."

The second Martian thought for a minute and said, "Yes—and that's only the top."

8. How fast can you go?

The **speed** of anything is the distance it moves in one unit of time. A car goes 30 miles in one hour. Its speed is 30 miles an hour, or 30 miles per hour, or 30 m.p.h.

It takes a motorcycle 20 minutes to go 12 miles through town. Is it breaking the speed limit?

Twenty minutes is one third of an hour, since 20 × 3 = 60. So the motorcycle is doing an average of 12 miles × 3 = 36 miles in 1 hour. Its average speed is 36 m.p.h. If the limit is 30 m.p.h. all the way, then the motorcycle is speeding.

R.I.P   *R.I.P*

*A learner was driving his car
When his friend said,
'You're too slow by far.
If you drive at this rate
We are bound to be late.
Drive faster!' He did, and they are!*

The speed of champions

You can probably walk fast at 4 miles per hour, and run at 12 miles per hour. This is what world record holders can do:

	Distance	Time	Speed
Sky-diver	—	—	185 m.p.h.
Sprint cyclist	200 meters	10.7 seconds	42 m.p.h.
Horse and jockey	1.5 miles	2.5 minutes	35 m.p.h.
Sprinter	100 meters	9.9 seconds	22 m.p.h.
Swimmer	100 meters	49.4 seconds	4.5 m.p.h.

The human body is not designed for swimming. You can run five times as fast as you can swim. But you can ride a bike twice as fast as you can run. That is because cycling is **efficient**. Very little effort is wasted.

Your biggest muscles are above your knees, in your thighs. Test it out. Put your feet flat on the floor, and push yourself to the back of your chair. Now, put your hands flat on your thighs. You can feel your thigh muscles going tight under your hands. It doesn't matter whether you're a hefty weightlifter or a couch potato. The muscles in your thighs will still be much bigger than any in your arms or the rest of your body.

When you run, most of the work of your thigh muscles goes into lifting you off the ground. Not much is left to push you forward. Running in place is no easier than running 100 meters. But on a bike you can sit down. The bike takes your weight, and most of the work of your thigh muscles goes into pushing you forward. Little effort is wasted. This is high-efficiency movement.

What did one bicycle wheel say to the other bicycle wheel?
"Was it you that spoke?"

Why can't a bicycle stand up for itself?
Because it is two-tired.

What do you get if you tie two bicycles together?
Siamese Schwinns.

Velocity

Speed is the distance covered in a unit of time. **Velocity** is **speed in a particular direction**. Ride your bike north at 15 m.p.h. and your velocity north is 15 m.p.h. Your velocity south is minus 15 m.p.h.

A runner who does one lap around a track may have terrific speed, but his average velocity is zero, because by the end of the lap he's back at the start. The total distance he has moved in any direction is zero.

You can tell how far away a thunderstorm is, using the speed of sound. When lightning strikes within sight of you, you see the flash in much less than one millisecond. The sound that we call thunder takes much longer to reach you.

Sound travels at about 760 m.p.h. This means that sound takes about 5 seconds to go one mile. So if you count the seconds between the lightning and the thunder, you'll know how far away the storm is. If there are 10 seconds between them, the storm is 2 miles away. If there's only 1 second, it's very close.

9. A change of pace

Have you ever been in a subway? When the train starts moving, there is often a terrific jolt. People standing up have to hang on, or they're likely to fall over.

You can feel the same effect in a car but it's less violent. When the car starts off from the light, you feel yourself being pressed back into the seat. You feel this because of **acceleration**.

Acceleration = rate of change of velocity

The light goes green. The driver puts his foot down. The car zooms off. The velocity of the car goes from 0 to 30 m.p.h. The car is accelerating. That's why the foot pedal on the right is called the accelerator. Press it, and the velocity of the car will change.

A tennis ball comes at you at 11 m.p.h. You swing your racket and bash it back at the same speed. The speed of the ball is the same, but its velocity has changed, from 11 m.p.h. to −11 m.p.h. The racket has accelerated the tennis ball, and changed its velocity by 22 m.p.h.

> What can you serve, but never eat?
> *A tennis ball.*

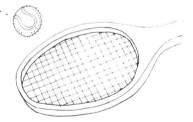

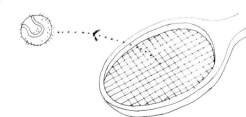

Slowing down

The light turns red. The driver steps on the brakes. The car screeches to a stop. You feel yourself thrown forward in your seat. Again you are feeling acceleration. But this time the velocity is getting less. The acceleration is negative. This is often called deceleration.

Newton and the force

Isaac Newton was a scientist who lived 300 years ago. One of the things he worked out was the link between force and acceleration.

| Force = Mass × Acceleration | F = ma |

When the car accelerates you feel pushed *back*. But you are not pushed back. The car is accelerating *forwards*, away from you. You will be left behind unless you are pushed forwards.

The car seat pushes you forwards. This is the force. The push from the seat gives you the acceleration you need to keep up with the car.

One thing that gives Superman such power is that he can accelerate to immense speed, without using force. Just by lifting an arm he can zoom into the sky. The rest of us aren't so lucky. We have to use force every time we want to change our velocity.

F = ma!

this must be negative acceleration!

CROSSES

What do you get if you cross Superman and a chicken?
Cluck Kent.

What do you get if you cross King Kong, Superman and a bug?
A 600-lb. cockroach that leaps the Empire State Building in a single bound.

What do you get if you cross a Model T car and an elephant?
Either a cranky elephant or a car with a very large trunk.

POLICEMAN: Why were you driving so fast?
MOTORIST: Well, my brakes are no good, and I wanted to get home fast before I had an accident.

10. Under pressure

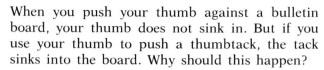

When you push your thumb against a bulletin board, your thumb does not sink in. But if you use your thumb to push a thumbtack, the tack sinks into the board. Why should this happen?

When you push against the board with a certain force, the board pushes back with the same force. Your thumb doesn't sink in. But the sharp end of the tack does.

That's the point . . .

When you use the same force to push the tack against the board, the board is not strong enough to resist. The point sinks in because the force is concentrated. All the force is focused in that narrow point. That means that there is high **pressure** at that point.

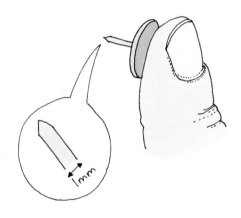

Look at the difference between the area at the top of your thumb and the area at the tip of the tack. When you use the tack, you are putting about 500 times more pressure on the board than if you just use your thumb. No wonder the tack goes into the board. It can't take that sort of pressure! *Remember*, you are pushing the tack with the same amount of force. But the area of the point is small. So the pressure is huge.

> What is brown, has a hump and lives at the North Pole?
> *A lost camel.*

The ship of the desert

For thousands of years desert tribes have used camels to help them travel across the sands. The main reason for this is that camels can survive for many days without food or water.

Camels also have big feet. Animals with sharp hooves sink into the sand. This makes walking hard work. Camels don't sink in. Why not? Their feet have a large area; so the pressure on the sand is low. Just as your thumb doesn't sink into the bulletin board, so the camel's feet don't sink into the sand. The camel seems almost to float on the sand, like the ship of the desert.

Snowshoes work the same way.

This elephant weighs 11,000 pounds. Each one of its feet has an area of 80 square inches.

A lady weighs 110 pounds. Her stiletto heel has an area of .08 square inches. If she puts all her weight on one heel, what pressure does she put on the floor?

> **Pressure = force (in this case, the elephant's weight) divided by the area that is being pushed down**
>
> **Pressure of elephant:** $\dfrac{11,000}{80}$ = **137.5 pounds per square inch**
>
> **Pressure of lady's heel:** $\dfrac{110}{.08}$ = **1,375 pounds per square inch**

Can you see why stiletto heels are banned in many public places? Would you rather have your toe stepped on by an elephant, or by a lady in stiletto heels?

HEAVY RIDDLES

Why couldn't Noah play cards on the ark?
An elephant was standing on the deck.

What do you get if you cross an elephant and a canary?
A messy cage.

What do you get if you cross an elephant and a Mexican dinner?
A tortilla that never forgets.

How much does a psychiatrist charge an elephant?
$100 for the visit and $850 for the couch.

11. Sizzling sausages

Sizzling sausages, boiling water, burning fire. These things are hot. Snow and ice are cold. We all know that, but scientists need to know how hot or how cold. And so they measure the **temperatures** of these things.

What is faster—hot or cold?
Hot—you can always catch cold.

Fahrenheit temperatures

Anything hotter than boiling water has a temperature above 212 °F. Anything colder than melting ice has a temperature below 32 °F.

Water boils at 212 degrees Fahrenheit (212 °F).

Ice melts at 32 degrees Fahrenheit (32 °F).

A healthy human body has a temperature near 98.6 °F. If you have a fever, your temperature may go up to 102 °F or 103 °F, but if it rises above 106 °F, you are practically dead. People who have had temperatures as high as 111 °F, though, have been known to recover.

If you get very cold your temperature may drop a few degrees. But you are in danger if your temperature gets as low as 86 °F. People have survived, however, body temperatures as low as 61 °F.

28

Thermometers

Thermometers measure temperature. With a thermometer you can find out how hot something is. A bulb thermometer, like the one shown here, is made of glass. The bulb at the bottom is filled with either silvery mercury or red-colored alcohol.

> What is the most educated thing in the science lab?
>
> *A thermometer. It has lots of degrees.*

To measure the temperature, put the thermometer in whatever you are measuring. Part of the liquid in the bulb rises up the tube—the *stem* of the thermometer.

As the liquid inside gets hotter, it expands. In other words, it takes up more room. The result is that it climbs higher up the tube. The higher it climbs, the higher is the temperature it indicates.

You read the temperature at the top of the liquid from the scale printed on or near the stem. The thermometer here is showing a temperature of about 176 °F.

> What can you measure that has no length, width, or thickness?
>
> *The temperature.*
>
> Why would you want to throw the thermometer out of the science lab?
>
> *To see the temperature drop.*

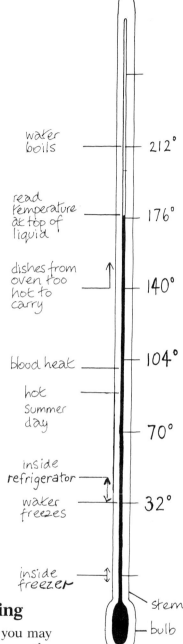

water boils — 212°

read temperature at top of liquid — 176°

dishes from oven too hot to carry — 140°

blood heat — 104°

hot summer day — 70°

inside refrigerator

water freezes — 32°

inside freezer

stem

bulb

But temperature isn't everything

When you eat cake with hot fudge sauce, you may burn your tongue on the fudge, but never on the cake. The whole dessert, fudge and all, may have been together in the oven and may all be at the same temperature. Then why do you burn your tongue only on the fudge?

The answer is that temperature isn't the only thing that matters. You also need to know that fudge can hold more **heat** than the rest of the dessert. We'll find out more about heat in the next chapter.

12. Getting warmer

Wow, Stephanie, is it ever cold today. I can feel all that temperature running out through my feet into the snow.

George, temperature doesn't move. Temperature tells you how hot things are. The snow is about 30 degrees, and your feet should be about 85 degrees.

That's what I'm beefing about. That cold comes freezing up through my boots....

No no George. Cold doesn't move. And degrees don't move either. It's only heat that moves. Wrap your hands round this *mug* and feel the heat running in. When the heat runs in that's what sends up the temperature.

Temperature and heat

On a cold day in winter you hold out your hands to warm them in front of the fire. What comes from the fire is **heat**. The heat warms your hands. Their temperature goes up.

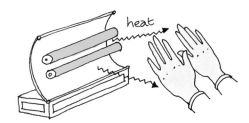

If you go out to make snowballs, your hands get cold. This is because the heat runs out from your hands into the snow. Some snow may melt. The temperature of your hands drops. They feel cold.

Heat always goes from hot things to cooler things. The heat goes from the hot fire to your cold hands. The heat goes from your warm hands to the cold snow.

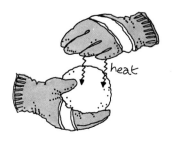

> *Remember,* temperature is a measure of how hot something is. To change the temperature you need to move some heat. Nothing can get hotter unless more heat comes in. Nothing can get colder unless heat moves out.

We measure temperature in degrees Fahrenheit. We measure heat in calories.

Traveling heat

We can travel by bus, car, train, or in many other ways. Heat has only three ways to travel:

1 Conduction. Heat flows directly from a hot object to a cold one. Wrap your cold hands around a warm mug of cocoa, and the heat is conducted from the cocoa into the cup and from the cup into your hands. This is **conduction**.

2 Radiation. Hold your hands in front of the fire and you can feel the heat. You don't have to touch the fire. When an object is very hot, heat will flow out from it in the form of radiation. This is called **radiant** heat.

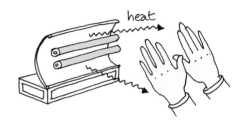

3 Convection. To warm up a room, you have to warm the air in it. A hot radiator warms the air around it, and the hot air will rise up. You can always feel the warm air above a hot radiator. As the air moves round the room the whole room is gradually warmed. This is called **convection**.

TEMPERATURE RIDDLES

What is "mean temperature"?
Twenty degrees below zero when you don't have long underwear.

DOCTOR: Nurse, did you take the patient's temperature?
NURSE: Why, no, is it missing?

With which hand should you stir your cocoa?
With neither. It's better to use a spoon.

13. Keeping cocoa hot

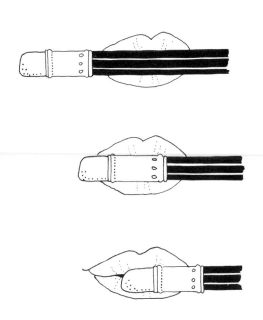

Take a wooden pencil with an eraser on the end.

Hold the painted wood against your top lip. How does it feel? Cool? Warm after a few seconds?

Now hold the metal against your top lip. Does it feel warmer or colder?

And last, the eraser. How does that feel, compared to the metal and the wood?

How can this be? The pencil is all one piece; if one end was hot the heat would flow along to the other end. It must all be at the same temperature. Yet the various parts feel quite different on your skin.

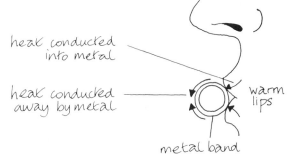

heat conducted into metal

heat conducted away by metal

warm lips

metal band

To understand what is going on you have to think not about temperature but about heat. The pencil is a bit cooler than you are. When you first touch the wood, heat begins to flow from your lip into the pencil. This is **conduction**. The pencil feels cool.

Within a second or two the heat has warmed up the bit of the pencil touching your lip. Wood is a bad conductor of heat; so the heat doesn't go any farther. The pencil suddenly feels warm. Where it's touching you, it is as warm as you are.

Metals are good conductors

But the metal band is different. When you touch the metal, it quickly conducts the heat away from your lip. Metals are good conductors. Heat flows easily through all metals. Because the heat is flowing out, your lip feels cold.

The rubber is a bad conductor. It quickly warms against your lip, and never feels cold at all.

Insulation with air is the thing
To make winter feel warm as the spring
So invest in a layer
Of lovely warm air
Trapped in holes tied together with String.

32

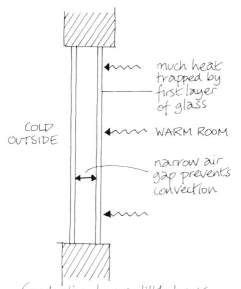

COLD OUTSIDE

much heat trapped by first layer of glass

WARM ROOM

narrow air gap prevents convection

Conduction low, so little heat reaches outer layer of glass. Heat trapped by the double panes.

Bad conductors

Bad conductors of heat include cork, wood, fabrics—especially wool—and air. Air is good at convecting heat around a room. But it conducts it badly.

That is one reason why wool is so warm—both for the sheep and for you when you wear a sweater. Wool traps pockets of air between its crinkly fibers. The air can't circulate to convect. It conducts badly. So inside the wool you feel cozy and warm.

The reason for double-glazing windows is to make a barrier of air to keep the heat inside the house. This saves on heating.

cork or plastic top is poor conductor

glass walls are poor conductors.

Thermos or vacuum flask

inner surfaces silvered to cut down heat losses by radiation.

gap between walls is vacuum. Not even air in here to conduct or convect heat.

Heat gets out (or in) only with difficulty.

SHEEP RIDDLES

NIT: How many sheep does it take to make a sweater?
WIT: I didn't even know they could knit.

Where does a sheep get its hair cut?
At the baa-baa shop.

What sheep plays with 40 thieves?
Ali Baa-baa.

The worst conductor of all is space—a vacuum. That is why the vacuum or thermos bottle is so good at keeping liquids hot. The glass conducts heat badly. The vacuum doesn't conduct heat at all. There is nothing to convect between the walls. And they are silvered, to cut down on radiation. Remember how heat radiates from the fire (see page 31). Silver reflects this radiant heat back to the hot liquid.

14. Why does a kettle sing?

Have you ever listened to your kettle? Next time someone at home puts the kettle on to boil some water, listen to the noises it makes. You get almost the same noises when you heat water in a beaker in the science lab.

Soon after the water begins to warm up you hear a faint hissing. The hissing deepens to a dull roar. Look in while it is roaring. You will see that there are lots of bubbles at the bottom of the water, but not many at the top. This roaring is what people mean by the *singing* of the kettle. This is the noise that is hard to explain.

After a few minutes the roar dies down. As the water begins to boil the roar changes to the sloshy, bubbly noise of boiling.

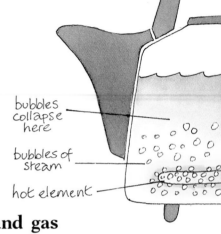

bubbles collapse here

bubbles of steam

hot element

Liquid, solid, and gas

Water is runny. It fills up the corners in the bottom of any container you pour it into. It runs out through any holes in a container. It feels wet on your fingers. It soaks up onto a handkerchief, a towel, or tissue. It doesn't sit around in lumps. Runny things like this are called **liquids**.

LIQUID

Put some water in the freezer and you can turn it into ice cubes. Ice cubes behave quite differently from water. Ice cubes are not runny. If you put ice cubes into a container they don't fill up the corners. They don't run out through little holes. They don't soak up on handkerchiefs. They do sit around in lumps. They feel wet only if your warm hands melt the outside. Hard things like ice are called **solids**.

SOLID

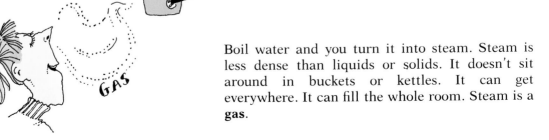

GAS

Boil water and you turn it into steam. Steam is less dense than liquids or solids. It doesn't sit around in buckets or kettles. It can get everywhere. It can fill the whole room. Steam is a **gas**.

You can't feel gases. They don't have edges, and they aren't wet. You can't see most gases. But sometimes you can smell a gas. Every smell you smell is a little bit of gas getting up your nose. Fresh bread, spicy cooking, and sweaty socks all smell quite different. But all smells are gases. Gases fill bubbles and balloons.

The song of the kettle

The kettle sings with a dull roar. You can see lots of bubbles at the bottom, but none at the top. That is the clue to the noise.

As each little bit of water gets heated at the bottom, it turns into a bubble of steam. Those are the bubbles you see. The bubble of steam is less dense than the water. So it floats up. But there it runs into cool water. The cool water takes heat away, and turns the steam back into water. The bubble collapses—almost as if it was pricked with a pin.

You can see hundreds of bubbles at the bottom. Each one collapses with a tiny BANG. All those tiny BANGs are what makes the dull roar. That is why the kettle sings.

Fizzy drinks

Fizzy drinks, such as Coke or root beer or ginger ale, have a gas in them called carbon dioxide. This gas starts bubbling out when you open the bottle or can.

Three states of matter

Solid, liquid and gas are the **three states of matter**. At home you can find many things which are in two of these states. A can of beans has solid beans and liquid sauce. A sponge has solid foam and gas bubbles. *You* are a mixture of solid, liquid, and gas.

15. Early morning dew

Early in the morning the grass is often wet. Walk on it, and your feet get soggy. You leave trails of dark footprints. This wetness is called **dew**, and it comes out of the air.

On a warm day the heat from the sun raises the temperature of the ground, and the ground begins to dry out. Some of the water in the ground goes off into the air. Damp clothes hung on a washing line will dry in the sun, because the water goes off into the air. We say that the water **evaporates**.

By the evening there is a lot of water in the air. This is steam—water gas—but we usually call it water **vapor**. Vapor is gas that is almost ready to turn into liquid.

How vapor vanishes

Water vapor stays in the air as long as the air stays warm. But at night the sun goes down. Everything begins to cool. As the air gets cooler it cannot hold so much water vapor. Tiny drops of water form from the vapor in the air. The vapor **condenses**, and turns into liquid water.

If the temperature goes on falling, more water vapor condenses. The drops of water may grow big enough to see. When they form on the grass we call them dew. Look carefully at the grass on a dewy morning. You will see that every blade is covered with tiny drops of water. Sometimes the grass looks almost grey.

DEWY AND DAMP

What did one dewdrop say to the other dewdrop?

"My plop is bigger than your plop."

Why can't you have dew two nights in a row?

Because there is a day in between.

What do dogs do in Turkey when dew forms?

Let it form.

A change of state

Solid, liquid, and gas (or vapor), the **three states of matter**, have various ways of getting from one state to another.

- Solids **melt** to turn into liquids. Snow melts to water in your hands.
- Liquids **freeze** to turn into solids. Water turns into ice in the freezer.
- Vapors and gases **condense** to make liquids. Dew forms on the grass.
- Liquids **boil** or **evaporate** to make vapors and gases.

Usually we say *boil* when we deliberately heat a liquid. We boil water in the kettle to make coffee or tea. But when water goes into the air from clothes drying in the sun we say that the water *evaporates*.

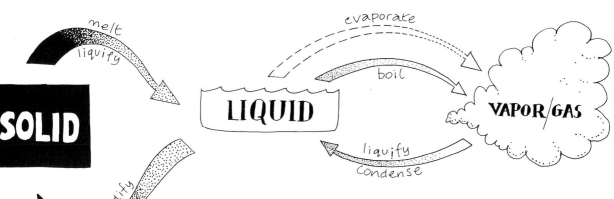

Three quarters of the surface of the Earth is covered with water, and this water evaporates when it is warm. So the air above the Earth always has lots of water vapor in it. When the air cools down low, near the ground, the water condenses as dew. When the air cools high up in the sky, the water may condense into rain drops. But more often it condenses into tiny little drops of water that are too small to fall down. They hang around in the sky, and we call them clouds.

What is the difference between a cloud and a spanked child?
One pours with rain, the other roars with pain.

If six elephants and two dogs were under one umbrella, how come none of them got wet?
It wasn't raining.

16. The air that we breathe

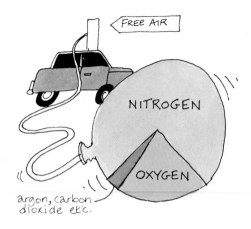

FREE AIR

NITROGEN

OXYGEN

argon, carbon dioxide etc.

Sparrows fly about in it, balloons and tires are full of it, and we can't live without it. But what is air? Air is a gas—or to be more accurate, air is a mixture of gases.

You can see from the pie chart that air is almost completely made up from nitrogen (nearly 80 percent) and oxygen (20 percent). You can't see either nitrogen or oxygen, nor can you smell them or feel them. And that is why we hardly notice the air. But remember, if it wasn't there, we wouldn't be able to breathe.

You want to stay alive?

What really matters to us is oxygen. Oxygen is the gas we need to stay alive. Without oxygen we could not burn coal and oil in fires and power stations. Fuel burns in oxygen to give energy. When we get oxygen into our bodies, we can use it to get energy from the food we eat.

Nitrogen doesn't do much. It is **inert**. That means that it can't help to provide energy. Stuff won't burn in nitrogen; only in oxygen. You breathe nitrogen in, and then you breathe it out again unused. But oxygen is different.

When you breathe oxygen into your lungs, some of it goes on into the blood. That is how you get oxygen into your body.

Carbon dioxide is a waste gas that you breathe out at every breath. In the gases you breathe out there may be as much as 4 percent carbon dioxide.

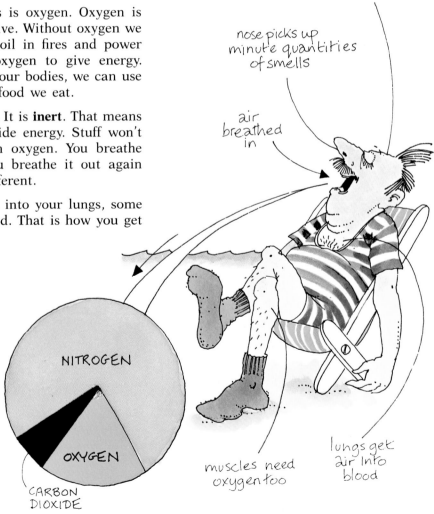

brain needs oxygen

nose picks up minute quantities of smells

air breathed in

NITROGEN

OXYGEN

CARBON DIOXIDE

muscles need oxygen too

lungs get air into blood

But you hardly breathe in any carbon dioxide at all, since in the air altogether there is only about 0.03 percent.

Air in funny places

You can't survive if you don't get enough oxygen. That is why some people have to carry tanks of air or oxygen with them. Divers who want to stay under water need to breathe. They carry bottles of air or oxygen.

Mountain climbers need oxygen at high altitudes. High above sea level the air is much less dense. On very high peaks the air is too thin to give climbers enough oxygen to breathe comfortably.

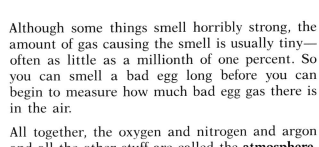

sniff

The other stuff in the air

Air has some solid things in it—plants and sparrows and bits of dust. It also has some liquids, such as drops of rain. But almost all of it is gas. Besides nitrogen and oxygen there is argon, a tame, quiet gas even more inert than nitrogen. There is a little carbon dioxide. There is some water vapor. And there are all the things we call smells.

Although some things smell horribly strong, the amount of gas causing the smell is usually tiny—often as little as a millionth of one percent. So you can smell a bad egg long before you can begin to measure how much bad egg gas there is in the air.

All together, the oxygen and nitrogen and argon and all the other stuff are called the **atmosphere**. That is the name for the air around the Earth.

17. Blowing in the wind

If you were a plant, you would want to get your seeds spread out and sown each year. How would you go about it?

Plants can't walk. They can't move about to sow their seeds. Human beings sow lots of seeds—carrots, beans, rice—but only the ones they want. If you were an unpopular plant you couldn't rely on human beings.

Suppose you were a thistle. It would be important to you to get your seeds in the ground. Otherwise, there might be no thistles around next year. You know for sure that your seeds aren't going to be spread about by people.

Why bother spreading seeds?

If you just drop seeds by your own stem, they won't do much good. For one thing, there probably won't be room for more than one plant in that spot. So out of all the seeds only one will grow. And, if you are still planning to be there next year, then none of the new plants can survive.

Besides, what you want to do is expand the tribe. Take over more land. "Build thistle power!"

So you have to get your seeds spread out as far as you can. Then with luck each one will fall on a bit of fresh ground that has no thistles yet, and start a new colony.

How to spread your seeds

Plants have found five ways to spread their seeds. The least common is by water. The seeds are dropped in pods—tiny "boats"—and they float away down the river or across the sea.

Some plants have explosive fruit, and fire their seeds as if from a cannon. On a warm autumn day you may be able to hear some types pop.

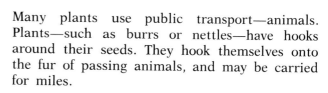

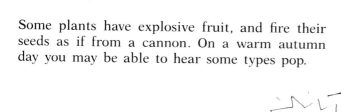

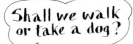

Many plants use public transport—animals. Plants—such as burrs or nettles—have hooks around their seeds. They hook themselves onto the fur of passing animals, and may be carried for miles.

Blackberries are delicious food for birds. The birds eat the seeds inside, and later the seeds come out in their droppings. Birds also like cherries, but they spit out the stones. Either way, the seeds get a free ride!

The fifth way that seeds are spread is with the wind. If you are still a thistle, that's how you would do it. Tie your seeds to a feathery parachute, so that they can be blown away by the wind. Some seeds are so light that they blow away on their own. Others make their own helicopter blades that whirl them through the air until they fall.

Theophilus Thistle, the successful thistle sifter, sifted 60 thistles through the thick of his thumb.

18. No lumps

Water from the tap usually doesn't have a very strong taste, but the water in swimming pools and the water in the sea both taste terrible. They taste so strong because of what's in the water.

Sea water is salty. You can taste the salt. If you swim in the sea and then lie in the sun to dry, you can sometimes see the white salt powder on your skin.

Swimming pools have chlorine in the water. Chlorine is a disinfectant added to kill the germs. It helps to keep you from getting sick.

There is only a tiny amount of chlorine in the water—less than two parts of chlorine in a million parts of water—but chlorine is strong stuff. Even that small amount is enough to taste, and enough to hurt your eyes if you get a lot of water in them.

You can't see the chlorine in the pool. You can't see the salt in the sea. Both the chlorine and the salt mix with the water completely to make **solutions**.

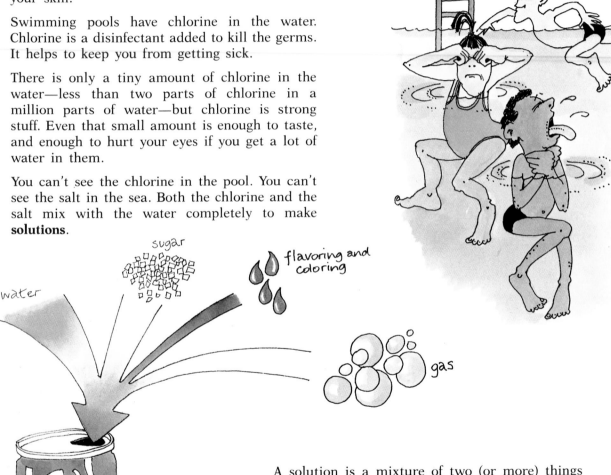

sugar

flavoring and coloring

water

gas

A solution is a mixture of two (or more) things that look and behave like one. Salty water is a solution.

Coca-Cola is also a solution. In the bottle it looks like just a single liquid, without any lumps or bits in it. Actually, Coke is mostly water, with some sugar, some flavoring, some coloring, and some gas in it. When you pour it out, some of the gas bubbles out of the solution.

How to make a solution

You can make a solution by **dissolving** one thing in another. For example, you can stir a teaspoonful of sugar into a glass of water. As you stir, the sugar seems to get less and less. Gradually it disappears, until there are no lumps.

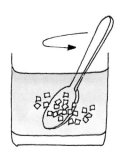

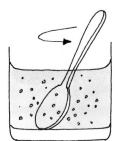

Look through a magnifying glass and you will see the little bits of sugar disappearing. They go soft at the edges and get smaller and smaller. When the lumps are gone, you have a solution.

After you have stirred vigorously for a minute or two, there is no solid sugar left. You have made a solution of sugar in water. It looks just like pure water. There are no lumps. And it's difficult to get the solid sugar back again without drying the water off.

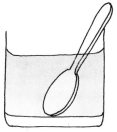

Dissolving and melting are different

Dissolving	Melting
1 You start with a liquid and something else, often a solid.	You start with one solid only.
2 The solid mixes into the liquid to make a new liquid.	You turn that one solid into a liquid.
3 You don't need heat.	You have to heat the solid to melt it.

What do you get if you cross the galaxy, a caramel mixture and a sheep?
A Milky Way baa.

19. How does a candle burn?

Candles are made of wax. Solid wax won't burn. If you tried to light it, the wax would melt, but it would not catch fire. So how can a candle burn?

Watch out for the wick

Running up the middle of a candle is a piece of string. It is called the wick. Without the wick the candle won't work. Does that mean that when the candle burns, it is really just the string that is on fire? No—string on its own burns quite differently. So the string and the wax somehow work together to make the candle flame.

Let's look closely at the burning candle in these pictures and see what is going on. Soon after the candle is lit, the top of the solid wax forms a cup. The wick comes up from the middle of the cup. The flame starts near the top of the wick. The flame itself is bright and white near the top, but bluish and dark below. Notice particularly that the flame is about half an inch away from the solid wax.

Do you see also that in the wax cup, around the bottom of the wick, is a little pool of liquid wax? Now we can work out what is happening.

It's only vapor that burns

The heat from the candle flame radiates down and warms the wax below. This melts the wax at the top of the candle. But liquid wax won't burn any better than solid wax. That is where the wick comes in. We know that absorbent solids will soak up liquids. A handkerchief or a piece of paper towel will soak up spilled ink or milk. In just the same way string soaks up liquid wax.

Once the wax has been melted by the heat from the flame, the string soaks it up. The liquid wax flows slowly up the wick.

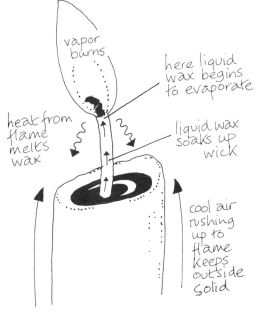

vapor burns

here liquid wax begins to evaporate

heat from flame melts wax

liquid wax soaks up wick

cool air rushing up to flame keeps outside solid

But how does that help? Liquid wax still doesn't burn. Before wax can burn, it must turn into vapor and mix with oxygen in the air. Then it can burn.

At the top of the wick is the flame. The liquid wax climbs up the wick getting hotter and hotter, as it gets closer and closer to the flame. The liquid evaporates, and wax vapor streams off the wick into the air. It mixes with oxygen from the air, and it burns. That is the candle flame— the wax vapor burning in the air.

Seeing the vapor

Here the candle is blown out with a sharp puff. The hot wax is still flowing up the wick, and for a few seconds you can see the white vapor flowing off the top of the wick into the air. It looks like smoke, but it smells quite different.

After the candle is blown out, we waited about five seconds for the air to settle down. Then we had a good stream of vapor flowing up. We lit it at the top with a match. The flame ran down the stream of vapor and back to the candle wick. It leaped through the air.

BURN OUT RIDDLES

What did one candle say to the other candle?
"Going out tonight?"

What did the candle do for sun and fun?
It took the wick (week) off.

How do they pay people who work in a candle factory?
By the wick.

Which burns longer—the candles on a birthday cake or the candles on the dinner table?
Neither. No candle burns longer. They all burn shorter.

Why did the candle go to jail?
Because it was wicked.

20. Ups and downs and vacuum cleaners

How do birds fly? They flap their wings, but how does this keep them up in the air? Why don't they come crashing down?

Because they push down on the air with each wingbeat, and *the air pushes back*. The force of the wingbeat makes more pressure in the air underneath the wing, and this extra pressure pushes the bird upwards.

push

air pressure increased under the wing

Hold your hand in front of your mouth and blow. You can feel the air pressing against your hand. That pressing of the air is **air pressure**.

Air is invisible. You can wave your hand· through it with no trouble. Sometimes we make the mistake of thinking that air isn't real. But you can feel its pressure.

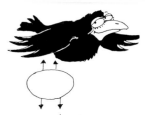

air at higher pressure pushing up on bird and down on ground

3–4 pounds

Living at the bottom of a sea

We walk about on the surface of the Earth, and above us is the air. It goes up for miles. It's as if we live at the bottom of a sea of air. The birds flying overhead are like fish in the ocean, and we are like crabs, scuttling around on the bottom.

All that air is heavy stuff. We often make the mistake of thinking that air weighs nothing, but this "sea" of air is miles deep. Your classroom probably contains more than 200 pounds of air. On every square inch of the Earth it presses with a force of about 15 pounds. That means there is a force of about 3 or 4 pounds pressing on your fingernail.

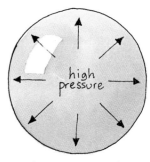

high pressure

Air inside pushes out equally in all directions

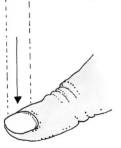

This force presses in all directions—not just downwards, but sideways and upwards as well. That is why we are not pushed down flat. All that weight of air does push down from above, but we can still walk about because air pushes up from below as well.

Why are bubbles round?

When you blow a bubble it forms a sphere. Bubbles are always round—never flat or square. One reason for this is that bubbles have more pressure inside than outside. The extra pressure inside pushes in all directions. The walls of the bubble are pushed outwards the same amount in all directions. So the bubble is round.

What's in a vacuum cleaner?

A vacuum is nothing. Empty space. No air. A vacuum cleaner has a fan inside that blows some of the air out. This lowers the air pressure inside. You never get a complete vacuum inside. But the lowering of the air pressure makes more air rush in from outside, and the air rushing in scoops up the dust and dirt from the floor.

dust bag

LOW PRESSURE

air pulled out

MOTOR AND FAN

air blown out

air rushes in to try and fill up low pressure area inside

You can test this yourself. Put the plastic nozzle on the vacuum cleaner. Switch it on. Put your hand over the end. (Use a piece of paper, if you like.) Your hand smacks against the end of the tube and is stuck there. The air pressure inside is lower than the air pressure outside. So the air outside pushes your hand against the end of the tube. You can feel the force.

VACUUM CLEANER RIDDLES

WICK: A vacuum is the dirtiest thing in nature.
WACK: How do you know?
WICK: Why else would they make so many cleaners for it?

Why don't witches ride vacuum cleaners?
Because they don't have long enough cords.

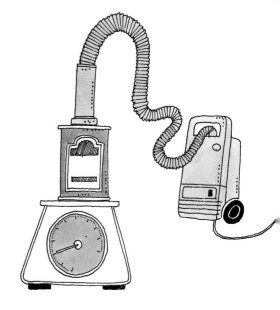

21. Depression in the bathtub

A **vortex** is a twisting spiral. A tornado is a vortex. You often get a vortex when you pull the plug out of the bathtub.

Try it—pull the plug out of the tub. The water doesn't just run straight down, does it? Often it glugs a bit. Then there is a pause. Usually a little dent appears in the water over the drain. Slowly, the water begins to turn in a whirlpool around this dent. Suddenly, there is a vortex—a spinning funnel of air down through the water to the drain itself.

Real Depression

When you pull the plug, the drain is the lowest point in the whole bath. It is literally a *depression*. The water above it behaves like the air in the vacuum cleaner (see page 47) when the pressure is low: the air rushes in.

First, the water tries to run straight in. But it is slow to start running, held back by what is called **inertia**. Then, when it does start running in, it doesn't usually run in straight. Instead, it runs in a spiral, like the wind trying to fill up a depression in the atmosphere. This is because of the spinning of the Earth.

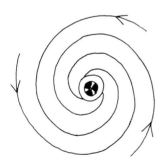

In the United States and Canada wind always blows the same way—counterclockwise around a Low (a depression). Usually, water does the same.

In Australia the spirals go the other way. Winds blow clockwise around a depression, and bathwater usually runs clockwise in a vortex around the drain. That's because if you're in the southern hemisphere the Earth seems to be spinning the other way.

Swirl around this way

The bottle emptying trick

There is another reason why bathwater runs in a spiral. The air can get out of the pipe, and will not get in the way of the water. That's why the glugging stops when the vortex gets going.

You can use this in a trick for getting water out of a bottle quickly. Take an old bottle, such as a large plastic Coke bottle. Fill it with water. Turn it upside down over the sink or outside, and see how long it takes to empty. Time it with a watch.

Now fill it up again. Put your hand over the end while you turn it over. Swirl the whole bottle around violently five or six times. Now take your hand off the top, and see how long the water takes to run out.

When you swirl the bottle you start the water moving around. Then when it starts to run out, it forms a vortex in the neck of the bottle. It looks as though this would slow down the flow. Less water can get into the neck.

But it does a vital thing. It makes a path for the air to get into the bottle. If the air doesn't get in, the water won't run out. Without swirling, the air has to **glug** in. Each glug stops the water dead. The vortex lets the air flow in and the water flow out—both at the same time.

Challenge your friends to a race of bottle emptying. But don't tell them about the secret of the vortex till after you win!

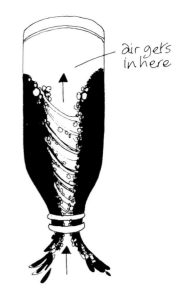

air gets in here

Check the bathtub, the basin and the sink in your house. Put some water in, leave it for several minutes to settle, and then pull the plug out carefully. Notice which way the vortex goes. If possible check each drain three times. When you add them all together, what percentage spiral counterclockwise? What conclusion do you come to?

22. Clouds and rain

What are clouds? From below they sometimes look grey and dull. From above, if you see them from a plane, they look like huge fields of fluffy cotton wool. From inside they look like fog. Fog and mist are just clouds sitting on the ground. They are all made of tiny drops of water—water drops suspended in air.

What color is rain?
Watercolor.

The steam from a kettle is invisible, but when it reaches the cold air a few inches from the spout it cools, and condenses into a mist of tiny water drops, or droplets. This is exactly how clouds are made.

Warm damp air is full of water vapor. The air stays clear as long as the water is all vapor, but if the water condenses into droplets the air goes cloudy.

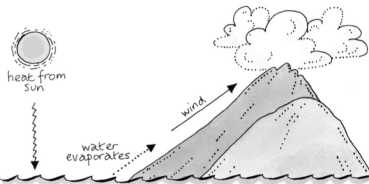

Where do clouds appear?

Clouds can be formed anywhere when warm wet air is cooled. Air gets cooler as you go higher. If warm wet air is lifted upwards, it cools, and clouds are likely to appear.

That's why clouds often appear around hills or mountains. When the warm wet air reaches the hills, it has to climb. As it climbs, it gets cooler, and clouds form.

Why does it rain?

Clouds are made of millions of tiny droplets of water. Sometimes those droplets come together to make bigger drops, and then they fall as rain.

What is odd is that raindrops grow bigger by not falling. If they fall as soon as they are big enough, then they will still be small when they reach the ground. But if there is wind rushing upwards, and this stops the little drops from falling, they can hang around in the sky. While they hang around, they bash into other drops, and get bigger and bigger. So the biggest raindrops have spent lots of time hanging around in the sky.

Getting the wind up

Hot air rises. Air expands when it heats up, and its density is reduced. As a result it tends to float upwards through the air around it, just the way a cork bounds upwards if you hold it under water and then let go.

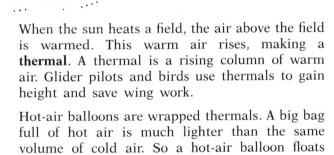

begins to rise and becomes a thermal

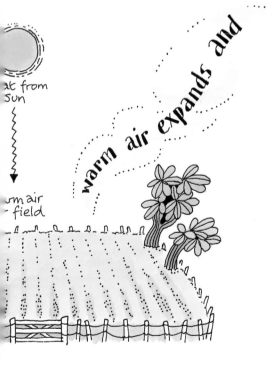

warm air expands and

at from Sun

m air field

When the sun heats a field, the air above the field is warmed. This warm air rises, making a **thermal**. A thermal is a rising column of warm air. Glider pilots and birds use thermals to gain height and save wing work.

Hot-air balloons are wrapped thermals. A big bag full of hot air is much lighter than the same volume of cold air. So a hot-air balloon floats upwards into the sky, carrying cargo with it.

Thermals begin over warm fields. If the fields are damp, and the air is damp too, then the thermals carry all that water vapor up with them. That is how the water gets up there.

What did the first raindrops say to the other raindrops?
"Two's company, three's a cloud."

23. Thermals and thunderstorms

The sun heats a wet field all morning. Warm wet air above the field makes a thermal—a column of warm wet air rising into the sky. Rising columns of warm wet air may make thunderstorms.

High in the sky the temperature is low. As the thermal climbs, it goes through cooler and cooler air. The water vapor begins to condense into droplets. A cloud starts to form.

The air is still rushing upwards. The droplets are swept up by the climbing air. They collide and run into one another. They combine to make bigger drops. As they get higher and higher, they grow bigger and bigger (remember that raindrops get bigger by not falling).

mmm..... Much like the electrical friction between snow crystals and raindrops.

It's cold up there

Strong upward winds, blowing at perhaps 45 m.p.h., carry these drops many miles above the ground. When they get high enough some of them begin to freeze into feathery crystals of snow. Others get so big that they begin to fall in spite of the wind.

The huge drops fall down. The feathery crystals blow up. As they sweep past each other there is "electrical friction" between them. This is why we get lightning and thunder.

Electrical storms are like stroking a cat. Sometimes when you stroke a cat its fur crackles under your fingers. This is a result of the electrical friction as your fingers rub the fur. In much the same way water drops and ice crystals can rub past one another to make lightning.

FLIP: That was some thunderstorm we had last night!
FLOP: Why didn't you wake me? You know I can't sleep during a thunderstorm!

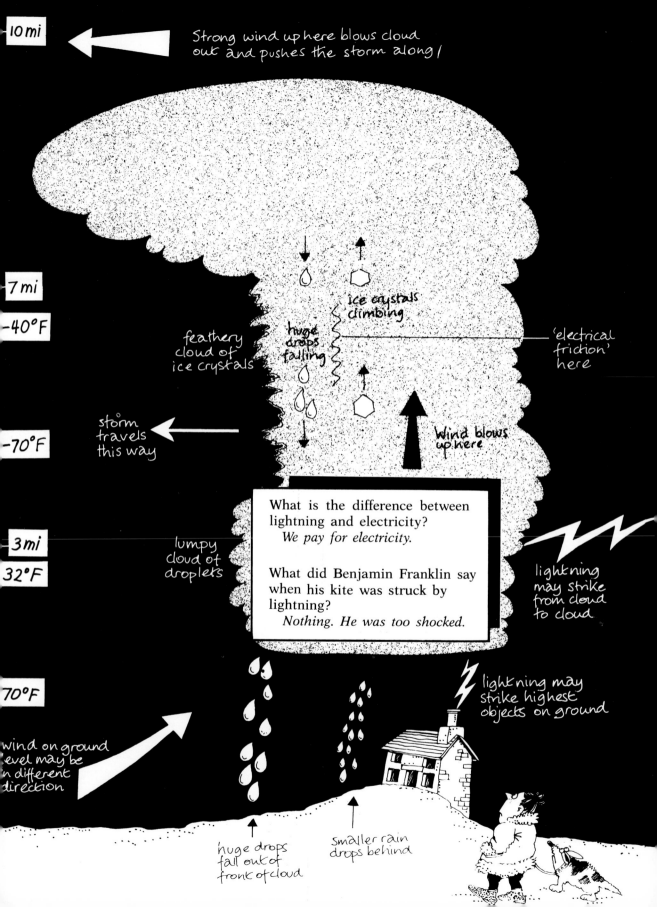

10 mi

Strong wind up here blows cloud out and pushes the storm along!

7 mi
−40°F

ice crystals climbing

feathery cloud of ice crystals

huge drops falling

'electrical friction' here

−70°F

storm travels this way

Wind blows up here

What is the difference between lightning and electricity?
We pay for electricity.

What did Benjamin Franklin say when his kite was struck by lightning?
Nothing. He was too shocked.

3 mi
32°F

lumpy cloud of droplets

lightning may strike from cloud to cloud

70°F

lightning may strike highest objects on ground

wind on ground level may be in different direction

huge drops fall out of front of cloud

smaller rain drops behind

24. Ice from the sky

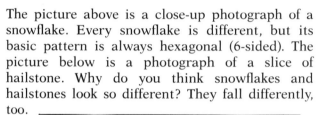

Where do snowflakes dance?
At the snowball.

The picture above is a close-up photograph of a snowflake. Every snowflake is different, but its basic pattern is always hexagonal (6-sided). The picture below is a photograph of a slice of hailstone. Why do you think snowflakes and hailstones look so different? They fall differently, too.

Next time there is a hailstorm, try cutting a hailstone in half. Can you see the layers of ice?

The heaviest hailstones ever were reported to fall in Canton, Ohio in 1981. A few weighed as much as 30 pounds.

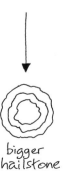

raindrop

↓ colder

ice lump

+ raindrop

wet ice lump

hailstone

+ raindrop

wet hailstone

bigger hailstone

Hail from the violent storms

In a thunderstorm there are violent upward winds. Warm wet air can be blown many miles into the sky. Sometimes, part of the water has condensed into raindrops, and is then flung high up, where the air is well below freezing. Those raindrops may freeze fast.

Fast freezing turns the raindrops into little balls of ice. They just solidify in the shape they are.

Suppose some of those round lumps of ice bash into the raindrops. The cold raindrops freeze on top of the lumps, forming a new shell around the old one.

The water drops freeze so quickly that little air bubbles often get frozen in. A large hailstone may have several layers of ice, with many tiny bubbles of air trapped inside.

Say this three times quickly:
Shovel soft snow slowly.

Slow freeze for snow

Now forget the storm. It is a cold winter's day. The sky is a yellowish grey, heavy with water vapor. The temperature is below freezing. The water vapor begins to condense.

Because the temperature is below freezing, the water vapor begins to turn into solid ice, but in this case it happens slowly. A tiny piece of ice appears first. Then more water vapor comes along, and more ice begins to grow on the first piece. It's not dumped on in chunks, as happens with hailstones. This time it grows slowly—to make **crystals**.

Crystals are solids that form slowly in regular shapes. They are often beautiful, as are ice crystals. When they fall from the sky we call them snowflakes.

What did the water vapor sing to the snowflake?
"I Only Have Ice for You."

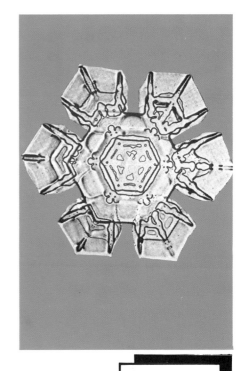

What is ice?
Skid stuff.

Frost on the ground

During a cold night the ground temperature often falls below freezing. If that happens when the air is damp, then the water vapor in the air may condense slowly onto blades of grass, twigs, and fences. In each place ice crystals grow, and we call them frost.

What lives in winter, dies in summer and grows with its roots upward?
An icicle.

What do you have when there's no snow?
Tough sledding.

25. What keeps a plane up?

Daniel Bernoulli (pronounced "Bernooly") was a Swiss scientist. One of the things he worked out was the link between wind speed and air pressure.

Take a strip of paper about 8 inches long and 2 inches or more wide. Fold it into a bridge. Put the bridge on the desk.

Now what do you think will happen if you blow under the bridge?

Okay—now do it. Blow down under the bridge. What happens? Does the bridge blow away or does it flatten down onto the table? What happens when you blow harder? Why?

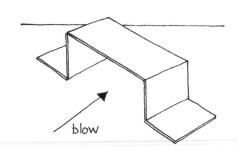
blow

High speed = low pressure

This was what Daniel Bernoulli worked out. The higher the wind speed, the lower the pressure. When you blow under the bridge the air is rushing through the gap. The speed of the air is high. So the pressure is low.

Because the air pressure under the bridge is low, the pressure on top of it will be greater. And so the bridge is pushed down. There is a force pushing down on the roof.

This link between air speed and pressure may not seem important. But it is. There is nothing else to keep planes up in the sky.

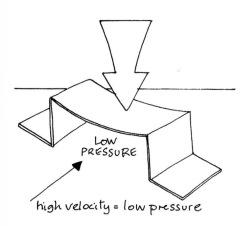
Low PRESSURE

high velocity = low pressure

Who invented the first airplane that didn't fly?
The Wrong Brothers.

This is a slice from the wing of a plane. It is called an airfoil section. As the plane flies along, the wings cut through the air. Some of the air goes over and some under, as shown in the picture.

Because of the shape of the section, the air that goes over the wing has to travel farther than the air that goes underneath.

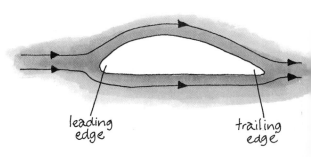
leading edge

trailing edge

So, if the air is going to meet again at the trailing edge, the air going over the top must move faster than the air going underneath.

But faster flow means lower pressure. So there is lower pressure above the wing than below. Therefore, there is an upward force, which is called **lift**.

There is always lift, as long as the wing is moving through the air. This lift is what keeps the plane flying.

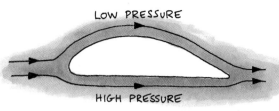

LOW PRESSURE

HIGH PRESSURE

LIFT

blow — high speed = low pressure

If you were to hang up two apples on pieces of string and blow between them, what do you think would happen, and why?

FLYING RIDDLES

What is big and hairy and flies 1,200 miles per hour?
King Kongcorde.

What do you call a giant frog that flies first class on the Concorde?
"Sir."

What happens if you cross the Concorde and a fat green frog?
A plane that makes short hops.

If one of your relatives thought she was a warplane, what would you call her?
Anti-aircraft.

26. Staying in orbit

A space lab is zooming around the Earth. Every 90 minutes it does a complete orbit—about 25,000 miles. The motors have been switched off. The lab is above the ground. Why doesn't it fall down?

Tie a roll of tape on a chain of three strong rubber bands. Whirl it around your head. Make sure you don't let go. What happens to the rubber bands when you whirl fast?

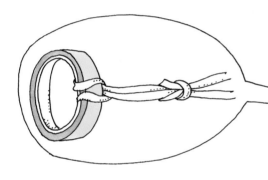

Circling

Take a look at the brick that is flying around in a circle at the right. At this moment it is moving north, up the page. But when it gets to X it will be moving to the right—east. Later it will be going south, and west. Its direction is changing all the time.

The speed of the brick stays the same. But its velocity is always changing. *Remember*, velocity is speed in a particular direction. Because the direction is changing, so is the velocity of the brick. Change in velocity means acceleration.

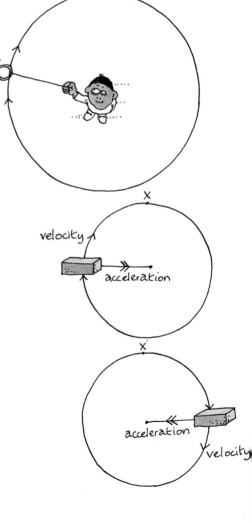

This brick is accelerating towards the center of the circle. It doesn't get any closer to the center, but it has to accelerate all the time to stay the same distance away. Just like the Red Queen in *Alice in Wonderland*. She has to run faster and faster to stay in the same place.

Anything that moves in a circle is accelerating towards the center.

What causes acceleration? Force. Why does anything move in a circle? Because a force is pulling it in.

Danger—high tension

What would happen if you cut the rubber bands? The tape would fly across the room. What keeps the tape going around is the pull from the rubber band. The force of tension in the rubber band makes the tape accelerate towards the center.

Some people say that the tape pulls outwards with *centrifugal force*. That isn't really what is happening. *You* have to pull the tape in. *You* have to create tension in the rubber band. *You* have to provide the force that keeps the tape accelerating inwards. *Your finger* is what produces the force— not the tape pulling outwards.

In the space lab, the astronauts seem to be *weightless*. They are accelerating towards the Earth all the time. So is the whole lab. The force of gravity is just enough to keep them in orbit.

tension ←← acceleration

SPACE RIDDLES

Who really enjoys being down and out?
A seasick astronaut.

Why can't elephants be astronauts?
Their trunks won't fit under the seats.

What did the astronaut see on his skillet?
Unidentified frying (flying) objects.

If athletes get athlete's foot, what do astronauts get?
Missile toe.

27. What's in the tube?

What is toothpaste? If you squeeze the tube, it flows like a liquid. If you leave it alone, it sits there in a lump, like a solid. Which is it?

A plastic liquid is a liquid that flows, but only when it is pushed. So toothpaste is a **plastic liquid**. Take the top off the tube, and you can wait all day for the stuff to run out. But if you squeeze the tube anywhere, then out it squirts.

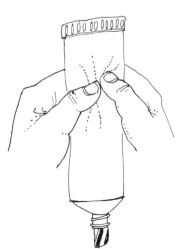

When you squeeze the tube you are increasing the pressure inside. Pressure works in all directions. It doesn't matter where you squeeze the tube—the toothpaste will flow out just the same. But a metal tube is much more likely to suffer metal fatigue and crack, if you squeeze it often in the middle. So to keep the tube together, it's best to squeeze it from the bottom. You can squeeze a plastic tube anywhere!

Sticky and springy

Toothpaste is sticky stuff. A bowlful of it would be tough to stir. If you get some on your finger it doesn't run off like water. You have to wash it off.

Toothpaste is also springy. If you hold the tube with the nozzle down, you can check this. Squeeze gently until the toothpaste sticks out about half an inch below the nozzle. Now release the pressure. Usually the toothpaste will spring back a little into the tube.

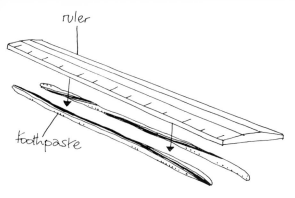

ruler

toothpaste

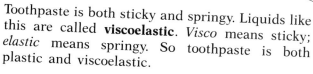

Or try this trick. Squeeze out a couple of lines of toothpaste about 4 inches long and one inch apart. Place a ruler on them. Now try pushing the end of the ruler gently. First, push it along the toothpaste lines. Now, across the line. Push and then take your fingers away. Does the ruler spring back a bit? It probably won't spring back the whole way, but it may spring back a bit.

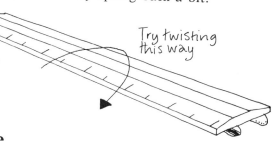

Try twisting this way

Toothpaste is both sticky and springy. Liquids like this are called **viscoelastic**. *Visco* means sticky; *elastic* means springy. So toothpaste is both plastic and viscoelastic.

The secret of the sauce

A few years ago special new paints appeared, called **thixotropic** paints. They looked like jelly when you looked at them in the can. Great sticky lumps came out on the brush, and they painted on like slippy liquids. A thixotropic liquid is like a jelly until you disturb it. Then it flows freely. The cans of paint say DO NOT STIR—because if you stir you break the thixotrope, and the paint runs and drips. As a jelly, it won't drip.

Ketchup is thixotropic. That is why it is often difficult to get it out of the bottle. It sets like a jelly. But with your knowledge of thixotropes, you can beat it. Shake the bottle hard before you unscrew the top. That way you'll break the thixotrope. Take off the top and the sauce will run out easily.

NON DRIP

What did one tube of toothpaste say to the other tube of toothpaste?
"Give me a little squeeze and I'll meet you outside."

What happened to the man who didn't know toothpaste from putty?
All his windows fell out.

28. Rub-a-dub-dub

Toothpaste is interesting stuff, packed with scientific interest. Some people also use it to clean their teeth!

Some toothpastes are clear, jelly-like liquids. Some are white. Some are blue. Some have stripes. But most toothpastes have some chalky grit added. So the paste is a suspension of solid in liquid, and this suspension is important when you clean your teeth.

Why bother to brush your teeth?

When you eat a mouthful of food, some of it sticks to your teeth. Whether it is potato chips or pistachio ice cream, some of the food will stay behind, coating your teeth with a thin layer. There is sugar in most of our food; so this thin layer has sugar in it.

Sugar is just the stuff that the bacteria in your mouth are looking for—a place for them to settle. They will camp in the sugary place and feast away. As they eat the sugar, they produce acid, which softens the hard shiny enamel on the outside of your teeth. Once the enamel is soft, the bacteria can get in and cause decay inside. Then you need fillings from the dentist, or, even worse, you may have to have the tooth pulled out.

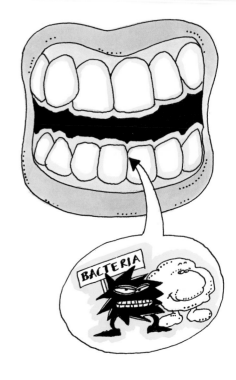

Clean teeth are strong and shiny. If you keep them like that, the bacteria will not be able to get through and cause decay. The point of brushing your teeth is to get rid of the thin sugary layer of food.

Just washing your teeth with water is no good. The sugary layer sticks too well to your teeth. Even the toothbrush may not shift it all. That is where the toothpaste comes in.

Clear gel toothpastes have a special detergent that helps to dissolve the sugary layer, so that it can be washed away. The chalky grit in most toothpastes works a bit like polish.

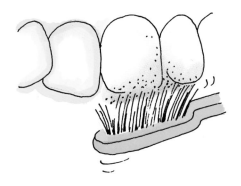

Down to the nitty gritty

With your brush you rub the chalky grit against the sugary layer. The grit is harder; so it scrapes the sugary layer away. But your teeth are harder than the chalky grit; so the grit does not damage the enamel of your teeth. This is called **abrasion**. Abrasion means rubbing something away by super-friction.

Toothpaste and a toothbrush are excellent for cleaning the lenses in spectacles, as well.

Sandpaper also works by abrasion. If you do woodworking, you have already used it to scrape away rough edges.

At an airport the landing lights must stay clean or planes will not be able to land safely at night. The lights get coated with a layer of oily dust that is not easy to wash off. They are cleaned by abrasion. A jet of compressed air loaded with crushed walnut shells does the trick. The crushed walnut shells are just hard enough to scrape off the oil dust without damaging the glass of the lights.

TOOTHY RIDDLES

How do musicians brush their teeth?
With a tuba toothpaste.

Why shouldn't you brush your teeth with gunpowder?
You might shoot your mouth off.

Why did the silly kid throw out his toothpaste?
Because his teeth weren't loose.

Why did the silly dentist throw out his electric toothbrush?
Because none of his patients had electric teeth.

29. Don't hold your breath!

The world record for staying under water and holding your breath is more than 13 minutes.

Don't try to beat this record. It could be dangerous. But see if you can hold your breath for **one** minute. Take one deep breath, shut your mouth, pinch your nose, and sit still for one minute.

Can you do it? Some people find it easy, but for others it is quite difficult.

The easy way

There is an easy method. First, take ten slow deep breaths. Each time breathe in as much air as you can. Wait two seconds. Breathe out slowly—as much as you can. Really empty those lungs. Collapse your chest. Make it tiny.

Wait two seconds. Then breathe in again.

After ten deep breaths like this, take one even bigger breath. Try to hold it. One minute is easy. Why is it easy? Because all that deep breathing helps delay a message from your brain.

Auto or manual?

Most of the muscles in your body are under your control. You decide when to stick your tongue out. You choose when to bend your wrist. But there are some muscles you can't control. Your heart is a muscle. You can't stop your heart beating.

Your lungs aren't muscles, but they are controlled by muscles that work your chest and the muscle that is your diaphragm. You can breathe in when you want. You can breathe out when you want. But most of the time you don't have to think about breathing. You don't have to say, "Time to breathe in . . . Time to breathe out. . . ." That is

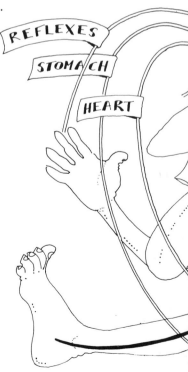

REFLEXES

STOMACH

HEART

all automatic. It happens all the time, even when you're asleep. That's because your brain decides when you should breathe, even if you aren't conscious of it.

How not to suffocate

Your brain needs oxygen. Without oxygen it will die, and so will you. Oxygen is brought to the brain from the lungs by your blood.

Now suppose the brain starts getting a bit less oxygen than usual. It sends out urgent messages to the chest and diaphragm, saying "Breathe in, you fools."

When you hold your breath for a minute, the brain will send these messages, and you will be forced to take a breath. That is why holding your breath is difficult.

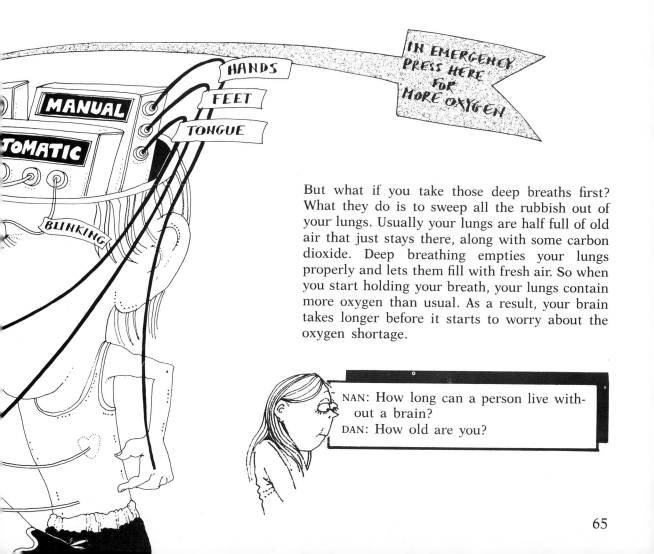

But what if you take those deep breaths first? What they do is to sweep all the rubbish out of your lungs. Usually your lungs are half full of old air that just stays there, along with some carbon dioxide. Deep breathing empties your lungs properly and lets them fill with fresh air. So when you start holding your breath, your lungs contain more oxygen than usual. As a result, your brain takes longer before it starts to worry about the oxygen shortage.

NAN: How long can a person live without a brain?
DAN: How old are you?

30. Breathing under water

If you want to breathe under water you need gills, a snorkel, or bottled oxygen. Let's have a look at all three.

All animals need oxygen. It is carried in their blood and gets pumped around the body. It allows food to be used, providing energy. Without oxygen, the brain packs up. That is why people die of drowning or suffocation.

What's so great about being a fish?

Fish have no lungs. They can't breathe air in, as we can. But they still need oxygen in their blood. They get the oxygen directly from the water.

The water in seas and rivers has air dissolved in it. You can't see the air dissolved in water. But when you *start* to heat a kettle you can hear it coming out. The first faint hiss, before the kettle starts to sing, is the air coming out of the water.

Instead of lungs, a fish has **gills**. These are like bony fans at the back of its mouth. As the fish swims, it lets water stream in through its mouth. The water runs over the gills, and out through the gill openings just behind them.

The gills take the oxygen from the water, and send it into the fish's blood. They also take the carbon dioxide from the fish's blood and let that out into the water. So the gills do for fish just what our lungs do for us—get rid of carbon dioxide in the blood, and put in fresh oxygen.

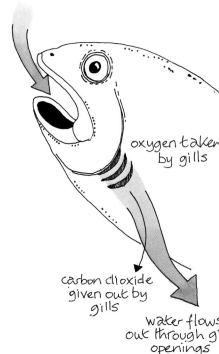

water flows in through mouth with oxygen dissolved in it

oxygen taken by gills

carbon dioxide given out by gills

water flows out through gill openings

Our lungs can't cope with water. If we want to go under water, we have to find ways of getting oxygen gas to our lungs. The easiest way is to use a snorkel.

How come fish get so much mail?
Someone is always dropping them a line.

Keep the tube short

With a bent tube called a snorkel you can swim along, looking down, and still breathe air. That means you can take your time to watch the fish, or look for treasure. You don't have to keep coming up for air.

When you dive down, your snorkel fills up with water. Then you must remember not to breathe in! Next time you come up, you blow out the water, and you're ready to breathe again.

This is just like what whales do. Whales aren't fish, but mammals. They have lungs. They have to come up to the surface for air. When they breathe out, the water vapor in their damp breath condenses.

What you can't do is try to go deeper by using a longer tube. Each time you breathed out it would fill up with carbon dioxide. And this is what you would breathe in with your next breath.

If you see a whale spout, it's really only breathing out.

Don't try this!

But there would be an even worse problem. You could never breathe in at all. Two yards down, the water pressure would be so high you could not expand your chest. Our bodies are used to dealing with only the pressure of the atmosphere. Two yards under water the pressure on the outside of your chest is 20 percent higher. Breathing in would be almost impossible.

That is why you need to use bottled air if you want to swim deep. You would carry a tank of compressed air on your back. When you take it down with you, and it's under pressure, then you can breathe easily. For deep diving you need special mixtures of gases and expert knowledge.

FISHY RIDDLES

What is the difference between a fish and a piano?
You can't tuna fish.

What is quicker than a fish?
The one who catches it.

What happens to a fish when it gets dizzy?
Its head swims.

31. Blowing hot and cold

Once upon a time the winter was so long and so cold that a Centaur came down out of the woods looking for food. He was half man and half horse and had never been into town before.

Don't worry, he's armless!

At the third cave he smelled something tasty. He stuck his head in and was amazed by what he saw. A woman was sitting on a rock blowing on her hands.

Why do you blow on your hands?

To keep them warm.

The Centaur wondered how this could be. Did she have a furnace inside her? Just then her breakfast came and the woman started blowing on her oatmeal.

Why do you blow on your oatmeal?

To cool it down of course.

The Centaur was so astonished that he tried to scratch his head. This was a mistake....

He knocked himself out with his hoof.

You don't need oatmeal

Try it yourself. You don't need oatmeal.

First, hold your hand 4 inches in front of your mouth. Blow a sharp blast, as if you were whistling. (No need to make a noise.) It feels cold and dry.

Now, hold the palm of your hand 2 inches in front of your mouth. Open wide. Breathe out a long, slow pant. This time it feels warm, doesn't it—and damp?

Water needs heat to evaporate

A cup of hot chocolate cools down mainly because water evaporates from the surface. This takes heat out of the rest of the drink. Water needs heat to turn into steam.

Water evaporates from the surface. This takes heat from the drink and cools it down.

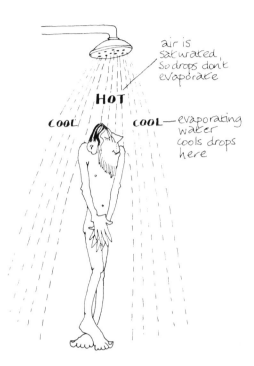

air is saturated, so drops don't evaporate

HOT

COOL **COOL** — evaporating water cools drops here

The palm of your hand is slightly damp with sweat. When you blow hard across it you help to evaporate some of the dampness on your skin. Evaporating the water takes heat away, and so your hand feels cool.

But when you pant slowly straight onto your hand, your breath, straight from your mouth, is warmer and damper than your hand. So the water vapor in your breath begins to condense on your hand. Your hand feels a little damper. And when the water condenses, it gives up the heat that was needed to evaporate it. The condensing water gives heat to your hand.

If you take a hot shower, you may notice that the water is cooler on the outside than in the middle of the shower. This is because the drops on the outside evaporate and cool. The ones in the middle don't evaporate much. There is so much water in the middle that the air is full of water vapor. The air is **saturated**. No more water will evaporate, and so the drops stay warm.

NIT (*calling Weather Bureau*): What's the chance of a shower today?
WEATHERMAN: It's okay with me, sir. If you want one, take one.

THE HOTTEST & THE COLDEST
The highest temperature ever recorded was 136 °F in the shade at Al' Aziziyah in Libya in September, 1922.

The coldest temperature ever recorded was −128.6 °F in Antarctica in July, 1983, at a place called Vostok, which is 11,220 feet above sea level.

32. Lung power

Did you hear about the time Mr. Universe failed? He was standing in a television studio with very large muscles and very small swimming trunks. He was invited to sing his favorite song while lifting 300 pounds.

He could sing the song (more or less). He could lift the weights. But he could not do the two things at the same time. He started the song, but had to stop dead when he lifted the weights. Why?

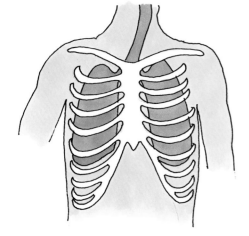

Inspiration!

Your lungs are like a couple of balloons inside the front of your ribs, near the top. Count down two or three ribs from your collarbone, halfway to your shoulder. That's where your lungs are. They are a bit bigger than your fists and pink and spongy. They are pink because they are full of blood. (If you smoke they may be brown and slimy.) They are like a sponge because they have to have a big surface area, so that the air that comes in can get to all the blood inside the lungs.

The stuff your lungs are made of is like very thin skin—so thin that air can get through.

To start with, you must get the air into your lungs. First, use your muscles to lift your chest. Expand your rib cage. At the same time you'll be lowering your **diaphragm** (pronounced "diafram")—though you can't see that.

What this does is lower the pressure inside your chest cavity, around your lungs. Because you make the space inside bigger, you reduce the pressure inside.

The pressure of the outside air is now higher than the pressure in your lungs. So air rushes in (as long as your have either your mouth or your nose open) and fills your lungs. You have breathed in. This is called **inspiration**.

Now let your chest go down again. Your diaphragm lifts. The pressure inside goes up. The air rushes out. You have breathed out.

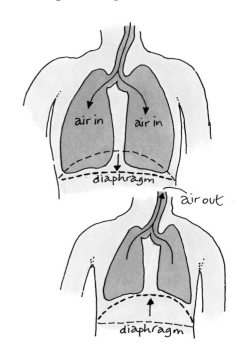

The trap door

There is a small snag. You have only one mouth. It has to cope with air for your lungs and food for your stomach. You won't have much trouble if you get air in your stomach, though you may burp a bit. But if you get food into your lungs, you choke.

To stop your breathing food into your windpipe, you have a trap door for safety. This is a flap of skin called the epiglottis. When you eat, it folds over the top of your windpipe to keep the food out.

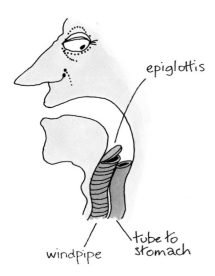

epiglottis

windpipe

tube to stomach

The Valsalva maneuver

But if you want to make a great effort you shut your epiglottis anyway. When you want to push very hard on something, or lift a big weight, you often grunt. What you are doing is filling your lungs with air and then shutting the epiglottis. Then you can use the high pressure inside to make your chest hard and firm. That makes it much easier to push or lift. This is called the Valsalva maneuver.

But doing it makes you grunt. When your epiglottis is shut, you may be able to lift a heavy weight, but you won't be able to sing.

Some tennis players grunt, too, when they make a great effort. They may raise a racket, but, luckily, they don't sing.

grunt

TENNIS RIDDLES

Why are singing waiters good tennis players?
They really know how to serve.

Why are fish poor tennis players?
They don't like to get close to the net.

33. The naked ape

There are 193 different kinds of apes and monkeys, and 192 of them are covered with hair. The only ape that is not hairy all over is Man. Most mammals are covered with fur—cats, dogs, rabbits—but not human beings.

The biggest piece of fur you have is on top of your head, where you probably have more than 100,000 hairs. Each hair grows about half an inch each month. Cutting your hair won't make it grow any faster, but it will get rid of the untidy split ends. As many as 100 hairs fall out every day.

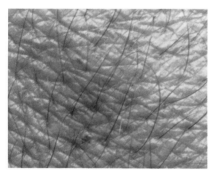

Follicles and roots

Look at the skin on the back of your hand. Use a magnifying glass, if possible. The hairs come out of little dents, called **follicles**. Each hair grows from a root under the skin. As it grows out through the follicle, the hair brings a little grease with it. This is why your hair can get greasy.

Long, greasy hair gets tangled and gathers dust. It looks a mess. When you wash and comb and brush your hair, it looks better. But it isn't healthier. All hair is dead, so nothing can make it healthier. After washing and brushing, the hairs lie smoothly side by side. They reflect the light, and so your hair shines.

Pull out one of your hairs and have a look at it. The root is the long lump on the end. Compare it

A head louse gripping a human hair.

Split end magnified × 320

with your friends' hair. (Better not pull out your friend's hair, unless you're invited to.) Which is longer? Thicker? Curlier?

Why aren't we covered with fur?

When a baby chimpanzee is born, it has a thick head of fur, but the rest of its body is almost naked. So people are a bit like chimps that have never grown up. Chimps need their fur to keep warm. Is our bare skin an improvement?

We have sweat glands on our bare skin. When we get hot, one way we cool down is by sweating. When humans first moved away from the trees, they had to start running after their food. Perhaps, in those days, they needed to keep cool during the day more than they needed to keep warm at night.

Head lice

Your hair is like a jungle—a great home for wildlife. Any one of us can catch head lice, and one child in every fifteen does. You can discourage lice by brushing or combing your hair every night, but if your hair touches the hair of someone with lice, they can hop from that head to yours.

When you have head lice, your scalp may itch. You may find the eggs or the "nits" in your hair. Nits are the empty eggshells of lice that have hatched. If you think you may have head lice, ask someone to have a look—a nurse, or one of your parents. Having lice is not dirty or disgusting. They often settle in the cleanest hair. But certainly you need to get rid of them. You will need the right lotion and the right help. The whole family needs to be treated to make sure the lice are wiped out.

34. Personal explosions

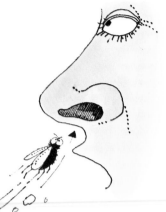

There are three kinds of personal explosions. Sneezes and hiccups are two of them. They are **involuntary**, which means that you can't sneeze or hiccup when you want. Right now you can't count "1 . . . 2 . . . 3 . . .," for example, and then hiccup. And usually you can't stop when you want, either.

Coughs are the third kind. They are partly **voluntary**. If you want, you can cough right now. And even when your throat tickles a lot, you can usually stop coughing just by deciding to stop.

Aaatishoo

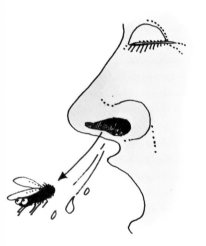

Inside your nose is skin that is very sensitive. As you breathe in air through your nose, the big chunks of dust are caught by the hairs in your nostrils. It is important to keep from getting dirt in your lungs.

But tiny bits of dust can get through. Then they may irritate the skin. The skin reacts against the irritation. You take a deep breath and explode it out through your nose to get rid of the dust. That's a sneeze. You have little control. The sneeze happens automatically.

> The longest sneezing fit lasted 978 days. Donna Griffiths of Pershore, England, estimates that she sneezed a million times the first year!

Sneezing is meant to be a self-defense system to guard the lungs. But sometimes it is set off by pollen. Pollen is the yellow "dust" made by grasses to fertilize their flowers. In the early summer the air can be thick with it on hot dry days. People who are sensitive may sneeze all day. This is called **hay fever**.

When you have a cold, the extra fluid in your nose may start you sneezing. The trouble with this is that your sneezes may fire the germs out at more than 100 m.p.h. The germs may zoom several yards and infect everyone in the room.

Hic

Hiccups are caused by eating too fast. Or you may have irritated your stomach with soda or something else it doesn't like. What happens is that your diaphragm starts twitching.

Each time your diaphragm jerks down, it yanks air in at the top. At the same time the top of your windpipe shuts, just as if you put a cork in.

Next time you're in the bath or have a deep basin full of water, you can create an artificial hiccup. Pull out the plug. Let the water run out for a few seconds, till it's running fast. Then jam the plug back in. The drain will give a *thunk* like a hiccup.

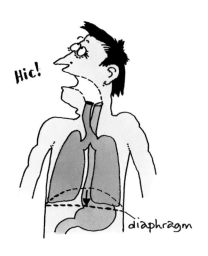

Er-hem

Clearing your throat is a good way to get rid of a little bit of irritating stuff. But if you want more power, then you have to cough.

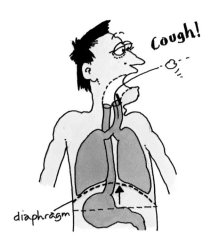

Sometimes you get a crumb in your windpipe. It "goes down the wrong way." Your breathing tubes have hairs in them, just as your nose does. They react violently to crumbs. You can take in a deep breath. You close the top of your windpipe. You build up the pressure inside. Then you open up and blast out the invaders. Less violent coughs are useful to clear your throat. You usually have some control over them.

> The world's longest attack of hiccups lasted 65 years, according to the *Guinness Book of World Records*, with 10–40 hics per minute. The victim, Charles Osborne of Anthon, Iowa, got the hiccups while slaughtering a hog.

35. Look out! The world is upside down

You can't really look out at all. All you can do is open your eyes and let the light come in. Your eyelid is like a bath plug. Pull out the plug and the water pours into the drain. Pull your eyelid out of the way and the light pours into your eye.

Green light comes from the grass. The grass looks green. Blue light comes from the sky. The sky looks blue. Your eyes use the light to make a picture of the world, and tell your brain what is happening outside.

Eyeballs

An eyeball is like a big squishy marble. Shut your eye. Touch it gently with your fingers. You can feel that it is round and soft. But don't press too hard—that hurts. And if you've ever gotten anything in your eye, you know how annoying—or painful—that can be!

Look carefully at your friend's eye. The eyeball is white around the outside. You may be able to see the thin red lines of the blood vessels that bring blood to the eye.

The colored part is called the **iris**. What color are your best friend's eyes? A few people have eyes of different colors—perhaps one blue and one brown. The job of the iris is to control how much light gets into the eye through the hole in the middle.

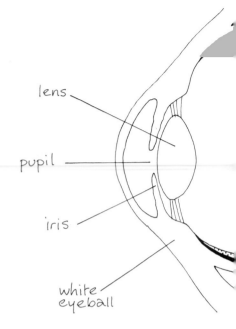

What have eyes but can't see?
Needles, storms and potatoes.

Which eye gets hit the most?
The bull's eye.

The black hole

The dark bit in the middle of the iris is called the **pupil**. It is just a hole, like a drain. The light from outside gets into your eye through this hole, the pupil.

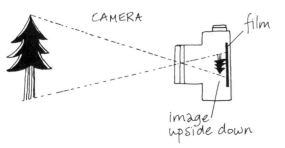

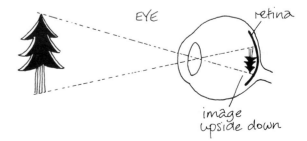

Your eye works like a camera. At the back of a camera is the film. At the back of your eye you have a **retina**. Here the light makes an image. The retina collects the light and sends messages to your brain, with a picture of the world you see.

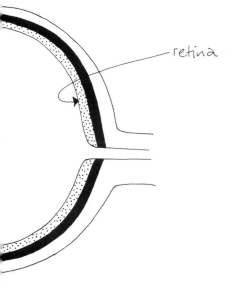

retina

Why is the world upside down?

The image or picture on a camera film is upside down. This doesn't matter. You can turn the photograph over. But the image on your retina is also upside down. You can prove it with a piece of paper and a sharp pencil.

Poke three or four holes in the paper, close together. Hold the paper about 4 inches from your eye, and between your eye and the window or a bright light. Look at the holes you made.

Hold the pencil upright, point upward. Move the point carefully up in front of your eye. Keep the point about half an inch in front of your eye. BE VERY CAREFUL NOT TO POKE YOUR EYE. The pencil may just touch your eyelashes.

The light from each hole streams past the pencil and onto your retina. There it makes a patch of light, with a shadow of the pencil point. These shadows, like the pencil, are point upward. But when you see the shadows, you see the pencil point coming *down* into the holes. You see the shadows upside down.

In fact, you see the whole world upside down, just like the camera. But your brain has learned to turn it all over again. As a baby you learned which way up things really are. So your brain turns everything over, and now you see the shadows the wrong way up!

What does a man with good eyesight see less of than a man with bad eyesight?
The eye doctor.

PATIENT: Doctor, doctor—I see spots in front of my eyes!
DOCTOR: Try these glasses.
PATIENT: Say, thanks—now I can see the spots much better!

36. The cat's whiskers

catstache

moustache

Have you ever thought about why cats have whiskers? All cats have these funny tufts of long hairs. They have one or two on each cheek, a few above each eye, and a bunch on each side of the upper lip.

What is cat fur?
Fur chasing mice.

The softest touch

Many people think that your fingertips are the most sensitive part of your body. They think you can feel the softest touch with your fingertips. It's not true. Reach up with your hand. With your fingertips, very gently touch the hair on top of your head.

Where do you feel the touch first? In your fingertips, or on your head?

Try this with a friend. Both keep your eyes shut. Touch the other's hair as gently as you possibly can. Each say the moment you first feel contact.

How do you feel?

You feel touch with your nerves. You have nerves all over your body, but most of all in your skin. The skin is the part of your body that's nearest to the outside world. So your skin is where you need to feel any contact.

Some parts of your skin are more sensitive than others. Hands and face are sensitive. You can feel any contact most easily there. This is because you have lots of nerves there. You have more nerves per square inch in your hands and face than you have in your arms or legs.

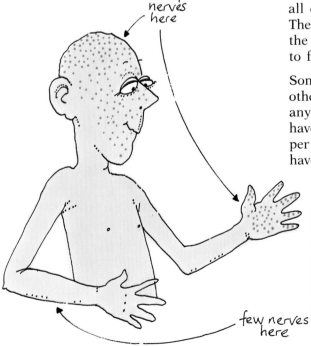

lots of nerves here

few nerves here

What do you call a person who doesn't have all his fingers on one hand?
Normal. Fingers are supposed to be on two hands.

Move quickly!

Help, it's hot!

What a nerve!

Nerves are the electrical alarm system of the body. They send messages to the brain to tell it what is happening. If you stick your finger in a flame, one set of nerves rushes a message to your brain to say "Help! Things are getting hot down here." Another set brings a message back to the muscles in your arm: "Get out of there. Fast."

But how can we feel with our hair? Hair is dead. Hair has no nerves. Hair can't send messages to the brain, even if it is nearby.

But, the skin underneath has nerves. When your hair is touched it pushes on your scalp. That is how you feel the touch. Your scalp—the skin on your head—is very sensitive.

The cat's whiskers

Cats are **carnivorous predators**. This means they eat meat, and they hunt. At least they are supposed to hunt. In real life most cats lie around sleeping, and wait for someone to open a can of cat food.

But if a cat goes hunting, then its whiskers help it to feel its way past obstacles in the dark. No cat will catch many mice if it keeps crashing into table legs and tripping over sneakers. The whiskers are the cat's distant early warning system.

tickle

Tickling is gentle, unexpected touching. Why is it so effective to tickle the back of someone else's neck? Why can't you tickle yourself?

What is the difference between a tickle and a wise guy?
One is fun and the other thinks he's fun.

What kind of tickle doesn't make you laugh?
A tickle in your throat.

79

37. Pins and needles

Sometimes you may have gotten a splinter in your finger. Perhaps one of your parents used a needle to dig it out. This may have hurt a bit, but often the splinter hurt more if it was left in.

Before your parents stuck the needle in your finger, they probably stuck the needle in a match flame. They may have told you that the flame would **sterilize** the needle and kill any germs on it. Otherwise, the germs would get into your skin.

Are you sure they are right? Germs can get into food, but why should they be on a needle? Needles are made of steel, shiny and sharp and clean. Well, take a look at these photographs.

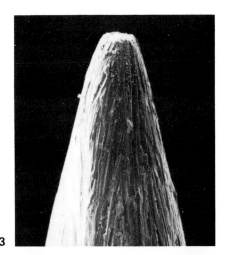

3

1 The point of a pin, magnified 5 times. This is what you see if you look at a pin with a magnifying glass. The point looks sharp, but not quite completely smooth.

2 At 30 times magnification the pin point doesn't look nearly so sharp. There seems to be a flat tip instead of a point. The steel looks less shiny and clean.

3 Pin point, magnified 120 times. The end is completely flat—not sharp at all. Down the sides are deep grooves, where the steel has been gouged away to make the point.

4 Giant close-up: 600 times magnification reveals an army camped on the flat end of the pin—an army of bacteria. These are the germs your parents may have warned you about.

4

1 **2**

If you pricked your finger with the pin in these pictures, some of the bacteria would get off the pin and into your skin. If they got into your skin, they might have made another camp there, and started chewing up your finger. This is called **infection**. Your finger would get sore, and might even go septic.

How to prevent infection

Of course, it's not a great idea to stick pins or needles into your fingers—or into your friends. But if you have to get a splinter out, do what your parents did. Use a needle (needles are sharper than pins). Hold the point in the flame of a match or a candle for five seconds. That will kill the bacteria.

If you cut or graze your skin, wash the wound clean with warm water and a little soap. Get help for any bad cut. What doctors or nurses often do is put some antiseptic on the wound, to kill any germs there. Then they cover the wound with a bandage, to keep other germs out.

Washing your hands helps to get rid of some of the germs on them. Wash before meals and you won't take so many germs into your mouth with your food.

SICK RIDDLES

What do you get if you cross a germ and a comedian?
Sick jokes.

Why did the germs cross the microscope?
To get to the other slide.

FLIP: According to a new scientific theory, exercise kills germs.
FLOP: No kidding! How do you get the germs to exercise?

Why did the sword swallower eat pins and needles?
She was on a diet.

38. Blue hands

Mm... this is just right

We think of blue hands as being cold. We say *blue with cold*. What we mean is that when someone's face and hands get very cold all the blood runs away from the skin. So the skin goes pale, and can look blue, in contrast to its usual color.

That change of color is not just for show. The human body is a cunning machine. There are good reasons for blue hands.

First things first

The part of the body that matters most is the brain. If the brain dies the rest has had it! So the body is geared to the defense of the brain.

Now the brain is rather delicate. It needs to have plenty of blood, with lots of oxygen. And it likes that blood at 98.6 °F. The rest of the body sometimes has to suffer while the brain stays warm.

When you go out in the snow, or jump into icy water, the body reacts with alarm calls sent to the brain: "Help; it's cold here." To which the brain replies, "Tough. But make sure I keep warm." And what happens is that the corners of the body are allowed to get very cold, so that the brain can keep warm. They are, if necessary, shut off from the usual heat services.

Heat is carried around your body by your blood. If your hands are cold from making snowballs, the blood running through your fingers will get cooler and cooler. This cool blood is unpopular with the brain. So the **capillaries**—tiny blood vessels—in your hands are narrowed down. Less blood runs through them to get chilled. Your brain is kept warm. But your hands go lighter, and bluish. If they are not rescued in a few hours, you will get frostbite.

The same goes for your face. Where it sticks out into the cold air and snow, your skin will go lighter. The brain is protecting itself by closing down the blood vessels in your skin.

You may be cold, but keep me warm.

Stay cool

When you get hot, it's just the opposite. The brain doesn't want to overheat. So all the blood vessels in your skin are opened wide. Lots of blood runs through. You go darker, or sometimes even red in the face.

You sweat; water comes through your skin, and evaporates from the outside. This takes heat away from the skin. (Remember the Centaur on page 68?) All these are the brain's tricks for getting extra heat out of the body.

People have been ingenious and clever in designing refrigerators, down parkas, and thermos flasks. But their own bodies are much more skillful at controlling the flow of heat. The brain is brilliant at heat control.

A house with central heating usually has a **thermostat**. A thermostat is a machine that keeps the temperature constant. It switches on the heat if the temperature drops, and switches it off if the temperature rises. That is what the brain is—a brilliant thermostat.

HANDY RIDDLES

What has two hands, no arms and is crazy?

A cuckoo clock.

What did the boy octopus say to the girl octopus?

"I want to hold your hand, hand, hand, hand, hand, hand, hand, hand. . . ."

83

39. Shivering fluff

Most people have temperatures around 98.6 °F. So do most birds. So do bats, rats, and alley cats. What do they have in common? They are all **warm-blooded**.

This means that all these creatures keep their body temperature constant. They have different ways of doing it, but they all keep warm.

Birds fluff up their feathers when the weather is cold. On a frosty morning even the smallest sparrows look big. When they fluff their feathers up, a layer of warm air is trapped around their skin. This helps to keep them warm. It's like wearing a down vest.

Most animals have a thick layer of fur to trap the air. We don't have fur, but we still try to fluff up in cold weather. What we do is get goose pimples, or goose bumps. This is our pathetic attempt to fluff up our fur. The hair we have is so thin and useless that all we get is lumps on our skin.

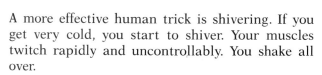

A more effective human trick is shivering. If you get very cold, you start to shiver. Your muscles twitch rapidly and uncontrollably. You shake all over.

This is another example of the cunning brain at work. Your muscles are not very efficient. When they work they generate heat. That's why you get hot when you run. If your muscles shiver all at once they will generate heat, and this will warm you up. You don't have to run—all you need to do is just stand in one place and shake.

What about the fuel bills?

Being warm-blooded is important, because it has enabled us to develop our brains. That has been possible only because we have been able to build a constant-temperature body to attach to them.

But there is a price to pay. Keeping warm is so important that quite a lot of the body spends all its time looking after the temperature. And, to keep warm, we have to find, eat and process food. Three-quarters of the food we eat is used just to keep us warm. Out of every four mouthfuls you take, three are used only for central heating.

That's an expensive way of keeping warm. All warm-blooded animals have to eat an enormous amount of food, just to stay warm-blooded.

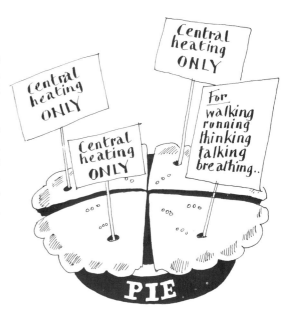

FOOD RIDDLES

What happens if you talk with food in your mouth?

You say a mouthful.

Why doesn't it cost much to feed a horse?

Because a horse eats best when it doesn't have a bit in its mouth.

What is the difference between a zoo and a delicatessen?

A zoo has a man-eating tiger and a delicatessen has a man eating salami.

What is the difference between a sharpshooter and a delicious meal?

One hits the mark—the other hits the spot.

What illness do you get from eating?

You get thick to your stomach.

40. Cold blood

Get up early in the morning on a weekday and you will see an amazing sight: hundreds of people waiting for trains in business suits, all facing the same way. But 250 million years ago there would have been something much more interesting. As the sun rose, the ridges of ground would be packed with dinosaurs. Every one would be standing sideways to the rising sun.

We think that dinosaurs were **cold-blooded**. Cold-blooded animals do not heat their own bodies. They stay at the same temperature as their surroundings. They warm up in the sun, and they cool down at night.

What's good about cold blood?

The advantage of being cold-blooded is that you don't have to eat much. While warm-blooded animals use three-quarters of their food just to keep warm, cold-blooded creatures use food much more sparingly. They eat much less. A rattlesnake is quite happy if it gets a good meal once a month.

But the cold of the night slows these creatures down. The dinosaurs could hardly move in the morning, until the sun warmed them up.

The heat we get from the sun is radiant heat (see page 31). This warms every square inch it hits. So for maximum heating the dinosaurs turned their sides to the sun. The fins on the backs of some of them were giant heat collectors. Just as you would hold out the palms of your hands to warm them at the fire, so did some dinosaurs hold out their fins to warm them in the sun.

Cold-blooded animals like the hotter countries of the world. You don't find nearly as many in cold places. In the zoo, for example, the reptile house is always kept warm. All reptiles are cold-blooded, and their warmth has to come from outside.

If you keep a crocodile in your bathtub, its temperature will stay the same as the bathwater.

What is a sick crocodile?
An illigator.

The good life—in Death Valley

Death Valley, a low desert in California, is made up largely of sand, salt, and rocks. Nearly 550 square miles of it are below the level of the ocean. On the sand flats there are almost no trees or bushes, almost no water, and almost no people. The phone book for the entire area has just a few small pages.

The sun shines all day, every day. Even in mid-winter the temperature often zooms up to 86 °F in the shade, and in summer the temperature has risen as high as 134 °F. People and other warm-blooded animals don't like this sort of place. They sweat too much and dry out. There isn't enough water, and there isn't any food to eat.

For thousands of rattlesnakes, however, Death Valley is paradise. They don't sweat. All reptiles have waterproof skins. They can't dry out in the sun, and they need very little water. Also, they need very little food.

SSSS

What is long, thin and goes "hith, hith"?
A rattlesnake with a lisp.

What did the boy rattlesnake say to the girl rattlesnake?
"Give me a little hiss."

41. Survival of the fittest

The animals and plants in Death Valley survive by being unusual. There is a little bush called the desert holly. It looks like ordinary holly, but the leaves are white. This bush pulls up salty water from the ground. When the water evaporates from its leaves, crystals of salt are left behind. The white salt crystals reflect the fierce heat of the sun away from the leaves. So the plant survives.

Fitting the conditions

Nature is shrewd. She knows that conditions vary from place to place and from time to time. So she provides a variety of plants and animals. Some of them must be able to survive.

In England there is a moth that is usually speckled white, but every generation has a few black ones. In the country the black ones don't last long, because they show up easily on light-colored tree bark. Birds eat them all.

But in industrial areas it's the other way around. The black moths survive. The smoke turns the tree bark black, and the white moths stand out and get eaten. The black moths are hard to see. They survive.

The black smoke does not turn moths black. The black smoke changes the conditions. With black bark the black moths are **fitter** for the place they live in. This is one simple example of **survival of the fittest**.

The **fittest** does not mean those who run fastest. It means those who best fit into their world.

Variation

Two hundred years ago no one could have guessed that black moths might become more common that white ones. No one can now guess what will make **you** fittest for the life ahead.

Look around. All the people you see are different. Some have curly hair. Some have blue eyes. Some have dark skin. Some can run fast. Some can scream loudly.

At school the best things to be good at are probably tests, whispering, and not annoying teachers. The color of your hair, your eyes, and your skin doesn't matter much.

What does matter is that there is a huge variety of people. Apart from identical twins we are all different. We look different; we have different skills. Any one of them could come in handy. Some pop singers make lots of money by screaming!

About one person in ten can roll up the tongue to make a tube. Could this ability make you one of the fittest? Well, suppose there were a worldwide flood of soup and we had to survive by swimming with our hands and sucking up the soup through a layer of liquid mustard. Who would be able to do it? Who would survive? Who would be the fittest? That's right. . . .

MOTH RIDDLES

Can moths cry?
  Yes, haven't you ever seen a moth bawl?

Can moths talk?
  Yes, they are always chewing the rag.

42. Whatever happened to the dinosaurs?

A hundred million years ago there were dinosaurs all over the place. Huge plant-eaters (herbivores) like brachiosaurus stood more than 30 feet high at the shoulder. Big meat-eaters (carnivores) like tyrannosaurus were as tall as giraffes and had teeth up to 8 inches long. Where did they go?

There were crocodiles, too. Crocodiles are almost the same now as they were a hundred million years ago.

Adaptation

As time goes by, conditions change. If animals are going to survive, sometimes they need to change too. We have seen how moths can actually change color to adapt to conditions. In much the same way, other animals must adapt to a changing environment.

Way back in the past, there probably were giraffes with short necks. As more and more animals wanted to eat the same trees, the giraffes with the longer necks had a better chance. They became the fittest. In the end, only the long-necked giraffes survived. They had adapted to the new conditions. **Adaptation** means changing to fit the new conditions.

Living conditions change over thousands of years. The animals that adapt are fitter than those that cannot adapt.

Extinction

Seventy million years ago there was a big change. Living conditions became difficult. We don't know exactly what went wrong, but the dinosaurs began to disappear. Soon they had died out altogether. They were **extinct**.

The problem may simply have been the weather. When we have a cold winter, we can turn up the heat. We can put on more sweaters. We can buy thermal underwear. And we are warm-blooded. That means that we can keep our bodies warm by eating.

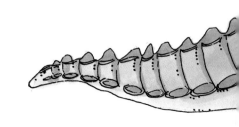

The dinosaurs seem to have been cold-blooded reptiles. When the winters got worse and worse, they became slower and slower. Remember, reptiles need heat from the sun to stay warm and lively. So, as the weather got colder, the dinosaurs would have found it more and more difficult to collect their food.

The crocodiles may have slipped into the water to keep warm. But the reptiles on land were in deep snow and deep trouble. The dinosaurs could not adapt to the changing climate. They were not fit for these new, colder conditions, and they did not survive.

DINO-RIDDLES

What do you get when you cross Tyrannosaurus rex and a witch?
Tyrannosaurus hex.

What do you call Tyrannosaurus rex when it wears a cowboy hat and boots?
Tyrannosaurus Tex.

Who is a little dinosaur's favorite baby-sitter?
Ty-grannysaurus rex.

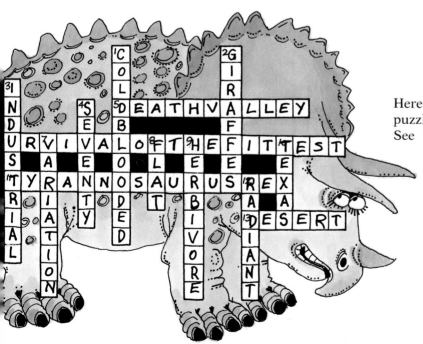

Here you'll find a dinosaur crossword puzzle with all the words written in. See if you can come up with the definitions, Across and Down. You can figure out all of this from the information in this book. Then you can copy the puzzle, ink out the letters and let your friends work it out.

43. The life that lives on you

The population of Planet Earth is nearly five thousand million people. On your skin there are more than five thousand million animals and plants. They live there. Your skin is their world.

Skin is amazing stuff. It's waterproof, and keeps in all your insides. It's flexible, and bends when you do. It's tough, and not easily torn or cut. When it does get damaged, it repairs itself. And all the time it flakes away at the surface, getting rid of dirt and rubbish. Meanwhile, fresh new skin grows from underneath.

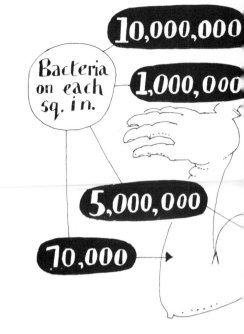

10,000,000

Bacteria on each sq. in.

1,000,000

5,000,000

70,000

hair

pore.

HUMAN SKIN

hair follicle

epidermis

dermis

Why aren't you sick all the time?

Not just your skin, but the whole world is full of bacteria. They are plants so small that—even magnified a thousand times—they would be only as big as pinheads. Many diseases are caused by bacteria, but you don't often get ill. Why? For two reasons.

First: Your skin is thick and tough, so bacteria can't get through. If nasty ones settle, they are soon swept off on the flakes of dead skin.

Second: Your skin is covered with *good* bacteria. They don't do any harm, and they seem to keep the bad guys away. All those millions of bacteria on your skin are probably protecting you from disease.

Three in four Europeans died

The human flea breathes through holes in its sides, and has its heart in its back. It can jump about 8 inches high and 150 times its own length. The bubonic plague, which killed off as much as three quarters of the population of Europe and Asia in the 14th century, is spread by its cousin,

the rat flea. The bacteria that caused the plague were carried by rat fleas, and injected every time the fleas bit an animal or a person.

There isn't much plague around now, but it hasn't disappeared. Human fleas are no longer so common, but many people still get bitten by cat fleas and dog fleas.

You mite be surprised

Just above your eyes there's a creature much smaller than a flea. It is a mite, and its name is Demodex. Long and thin, it lives in the follicles of your eyelashes. Luckily, it doesn't seem to do much harm. Your best defense against Demodex, and against the bacteria that cause acne, is plenty of soap and water.

All these things that live on us are called parasites. Dogs have parasites. Cats have parasites. Even parasites have parasites.

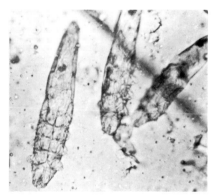

Demodex

FLEA RIDDLES

Does Bo Peep have fleas?
No, all her fleas are on the lam.

How do you feel when you have a sore throat and fleas?
Hoarse and buggy.

Why was the mother flea so sad?
Because her children were going to the dogs.

How is a dog different from a flea?
A dog can have fleas, but a flea can't have dogs.

44. Superbrain

MNEMOSYNE

Do you ever forget things? Everybody does. We are all sometimes a bit absent-minded. Would you like to remember everything? To remember really well, what you need are tricks.

A **mnemonic** (pronounced "ne-*mon*-ic") is a trick to help you remember something. Professional memory artists use mnemonics all the time. Here is a simple one: "Thirty days hath September, April, June and November. . . ."

How to stick memories together

No one knows exactly how the brain works. We do know that we remember things best in groups. You can recall your multiplication tables partly because they are groups of numbers. A good group makes a mnemonic.

> Mnemosyne (pronounced Ne-*moss*-inny) was the goddess of memory in Greek mythology. She was also the mother of the nine Muses.

1 is a BUN

2 is a SHOE

3 is a TREE

4 is a DOOR

5 is a HIVE

6 is STICKS

7 is HEAVEN

8 is a GATE

9 is a MINE

10 is a PEN

The one-is-a-bun trick

Here is a wonderful mnemonic trick. Learn these numbers and pictures. Read the list through four times. Say it aloud if you can. Practice saying the list until no one can trip you up. Once you know it, you will have a mnemonic you can use to amaze everyone. You will remember the shopping list. You will be able to recite the top ten in the charts. You can use your One-Is-a-Bun list to remember any other list of ten things. All you need to do is group the two lists in pairs. Suppose there are these ten things:

| 1 Cow | 2 Cabbage | 3 Ladder | 4 Pencil | 5 Fire-engine |
| 6 Cup | 7 Bicycle | 8 Cat | 9 Fish sticks | 10 Teacher |

When you see this new list, don't try and remember that 1 is a cow. You know that **1 is a bun**. So connect the cow and the bun. Make up a silly picture in your head of a cow and a bun together. A cow eating a bun . . . or a cow shut in a giant bun, like a mooing hamburger . . . or a cow standing up on top of a huge sticky bun. The sillier the picture, the better.

As soon as you have made up a picture, go on to the next. **2 is a shoe**. How about a cabbage stuffed into a shoe . . . or someone trying to clean a pair of shoes with a cabbage?

3 is a tree. A ladder up a tree is easy—but you will remember a silly picture better. How about a tree climbing a ladder?

You will need about 20 seconds to connect each word with the One-Is-a-Bun list. When you get to the end, you will find you can remember the whole list easily. You can recite it backwards. You can recall number 5, or any other number. Everyone will think you have a superbrain!

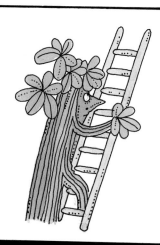

FORGETTABLE JOKES

FLIP: My mother has the worst memory in the world.
FLOP: She forgets everything?
FLIP: No, she remembers everything.

What do you get when you cross an absent-minded professor with a flea?
A forget-me-nit.

MOE: I saw a doctor today about my memory.
FLO: What did he do?
MOE: I can't remember, but he made me pay in advance.

Index